AF488269

VISUAL POETRY OF JAPAN

//1684–2023/

Asemic Writing
Calligrams
Calligraphy
Collages
Concrete Poems
Haiku
Japanese Translations
Lexical Poems
Mail Art
Photography
Visual Poems

Edited by
TAYLOR MIGNON

Coedited & Designed by
RICK ELIZAGA

Introduction by
ANDREW CAMPANA

Visual Poetry of Japan: 1684–2023

Edited by
Taylor Mignon

Coedited & Designed by
Rick Elizaga

Advisors
Shikama Hiroko
John Solt

Introduction by
Andrew Campana

Special thanks to
Matthew Chozick (Awai Books)
Nakagawa Haru
Nodomi Akane
Paul Rossiter (Isobar Press)
Barbara Summerhawk (TPJ)
& Ted Taylor

ISBN 979-8-218-31882-6

Published by
KERPLUNK!
unexpected books
related to Japan

front cover and title page:
Sculpture of the Buddhist monk Kūya
Late Kamakura period (ca. 1200)
with photo manipulation by Shikama Hiroko and Rick Elizaga

back cover:
Op. 022
Tsuji Setsuko, 1969
(also appears on p. 20)

CONTENTS

top: detail of "View from a Balcony of an Early Summer Street," by Hagiwara Kyōjirō, 1925

新

聲

新しき聲

新聲

BRU・・・・・・UNBB聲

塔塔塔塔人人人人人

ベルの聲人人人

S

バベルの塔

新聲聲山谷山バベル塔踊る人

聲聲+バベルの塔

聲+心のなかを耕す人

聲聲・塔・・・・・耕す人戀人

聲+++聲+耕す人人人戀人

物聲VON BBBBB聲

聲VON BBBB聲聲飛行機

聲NR BBB曙の聲聲聲聲

INTRODUCTION

BY ANDREW CAMPANA

Growing up in Toronto, my high school was right next to a small street called "bpNichol lane;" the odd capitalization and lack of spaces always caught my eye. Eventually, I found out that the street's namesake was one of Canada's most celebrated experimental sound, visual, and performance poets. bpNichol's "Pome Poem" from 1972 is a performance piece that forever shaped how I understood what poetry was or what it could be: from its opening declaration of "What is a poem is inside of your body body body body" to its hushed fading out with "What is a poem *is inside of your breathing breathing breathing breathing*." It is this that immediately came to mind when seeing the striking Kamakura period sculpture of the monk Kūya on the cover of this book, with six tiny manifestations of the buddha Amida emerging from his mouth, each of which is simultaneously a transcendental being, a divine force, a crafted figure, a word in the *nembutsu* chant, a vocalization, and a breath, all coming together with tremendous poetic force.

The volume you're about to dive into, *Visual Poetry of Japan: 1684–2023*, has been so necessary for so long. That it exists, and that it encompasses so many diverse types of practice—as stated on the cover, asemic writing, calligrams, calligraphy, collages, concrete poems, haiku, Japanese translations, lexical poems, mail art, photography, and visual poems—is a miracle. There is a conventional idea of what "poetry" is and how it's consumed: in printed books and journals, each poem with identical formatting, and if you're lucky, you might hear the poet read their work aloud in a café or a community center with a certain kind of acceptable "poet voice." But there are so many other kinds of poetry that do not fit at all into this model—ones that can't neatly be captured on the page, or at least gesture powerfully beyond it, and require other kinds of engagement entirely.

Visual poetry, in the expanded sense that it is presented here, has always been central to the story of poetry in Japan, but has remained criminally underrepresented in collections and anthologies, both in Japanese and in translation, not fitting into the normative idea of what a "poem" is supposed to be or look like. If they receive attention at all, they're often framed as novelties, as unconnected one-off experiments from different eras, as the sideshow but never the main event. This volume argues otherwise. Sometimes the curatorial gesture of putting such disparate works together results in a kind of implicit notion that we should consider everything to be just different manifestations of the same idea across time, resulting in a kind of flattening out. But what we have here is something much more nuanced, and much more exciting—there are resonances across the hundreds of years of visual poetry represented here, but also enormous gaps, productive dissonances, and irresolvable juxtapositions. These are singular works allowed to exist both singularly and alongside one another.

In Japan, before the modern era, it would have been absurd to consider poetry as something at all separate from visuality. Text was inextricable from its materials; each poem came into being at the nexus of some combination of ink, gesture, brush, and paper, or even chisel and stone, or stylus and clay. While poems were of course anthologized into written and eventually printed collections—many sponsored by the imperial court—those were just one node in a vast network of practices. Poems were composed to be sung; to be pitched against one another in *uta-awase* poetry competitions; to be incorporated into theatrical performances and rituals; to be carved into stone monuments (the *bussokusekika*, "Buddha Foot Stone Poem," was an early Nara period poetry form specifically designed for this); and to be carefully calligraphed or scrawled hastily on all manner of paper scraps, fans, screens, cups, sword guards, hanging scrolls, and more. Poems also jostled alongside illustrations, were nestled into ink paintings, and danced around the embellishments of decorative paper; the haiku-accompanying *haiga* ink drawings, one of which is in this volume, are not mere accompaniments to a poem but are wordless rearticulations of the poem itself. Visuality was even more important for the earliest "Japanese" texts, written in *man'yō-gana*—a precursor to the kana syllabaries we know today, where one chose from a vast variety of Chinese characters to render the sounds of the Japanese language. This was well before the standardization of certain kanji to the exclusion of all others, and before *hiragana* and *katakana* as we know them, so the choice of characters was far more open and less predetermined, and thus became yet another powerful tool of visual expression.

The Meiji era saw a shift towards printed poetry books—many of which featured an all-new poetic form, the *shintaishi* of the late 19th century, which eventually became the free verse poem simply called *shi*—with poems rendered in regular moveable type, and with far fewer non-textual visual elements than before. The modernist poetry of the 1920s and 1930s—the Taishō and early Shōwa—took many different turns away from this. This was a time of intense grappling with global avant-garde movements across art forms, including Dada, Surrealism, Futurism, and many more works hard to pin down into any given category. Poets represented here like Hirato Renkichi and Hagiwara Kyōjiro created poems that exploded across the page in multiple directions, mixing languages and symbols and geometric layouts to capture the poetics of a new era—a poetry that spoke simultaneously to the depths of the human psyche plumbed by cutting-edge psychoanalytic techniques, the new visualities, auralities and temporalities of the cinema and radio, and even the speed and violence of modern mechanized warfare.

After World War II, experimental associations and collectives—many of which were inspired by these earlier modernist works—assembled and reassembled, creating a blossoming of visual, sound, and performance poetry the likes which had never been seen before or since. Poetry became the key way to find new kinds of expression in the wake of the horror of

the prior decades, and for the boundaries
between media and artistic disciplines to
fall away, a phenomenon later referred
to as "intermedia" (a term popularized
by Dick Higgins of Fluxus). The 1950s
and 1960s saw poetic practices in every
imaginable configuration of form and
medium: to name just a few, Kitasono

Katué's photographs of assemblages of objects he called plastic poems (*pu-rasutikku poemu*); Niikuni Seiichi's concrete poems (*gutaishi*) and phonetic
poems (*onseishi*); Fujitomi Yasuo's concrete poems; Yoko Ono's instruc-
tional poems; Akiyama Kuniharu's tape recorder poems (*tēpu rekōdā no
tame no shi*); Jikken Kōbō's autoslide poems; Matsumoto Toshio's docu-
mentary poems; Kanno Seiko's semiotic poems (*kigōshi*); Shiomi Mieko's
spatial poems; and musical poetic dramas (*ongaku shigeki*) by creators like
Moroi Makoto and Abe Kōbō.

When I describe this long history of premodern poetry inextrica-
ble from visuality, and then move to talking about visual modernist and
postwar experiments of the 20th century that continue to echo today, I do
not wish to say that modernist and contemporary experiments with visual
poetry in Japan—many of which are represented within these pages—were
some sort of "return" to an older tradition of foregrounding poetry's
visuality. That doesn't do justice to just how interesting these newer
experiments were, nor how diverse the poets' motivations to create them.
Rather, I bring up these earlier echoes and this transtemporal narrative
to emphasize that the conventional idea of poetry—as something page-

bound and mostly occurring in books or
journals, typeset into regular lines, and
visual only in their choice of words and
lineation on the page—is itself a historical
anomaly, a blip. Poetry *is* something across
media, and always has been. Poetry *is* visual
poetry; poetry *is* sound poetry; poetry *is*
performance poetry. In other words, it's

top: semiotic poem by Kanno Seiko
left: book cover of *Grapefruit* by Yoko Ono

"printed text poetry" that should be the side-phenomenon with its own name, not the other stuff.

I want to linger a bit longer on just one specific figure, as an example of the many facets and ethical stakes of this kind of work. Niikuni Seiichi is, rightfully, one of the first names that come to mind when it comes to visual poetry in Japan—in his case, concrete poetry (*gutaishi*). His first collection, 1963's *Zero Sound* (*Zero-on*) took advantage of new developments in phototypesetting that allowed for incredible freedom in placing characters on the page, allowing one to change their orientation and size and to distort their shape. Half of the book is dedicated to visual poems, spindly lines of poetic text wriggling across the page; the other half is "sonic poems" or "phonetic poems" (*onkyo-shi* or *onsei-shi*), some of which we are lucky enough to have recordings of Niikuni himself reading

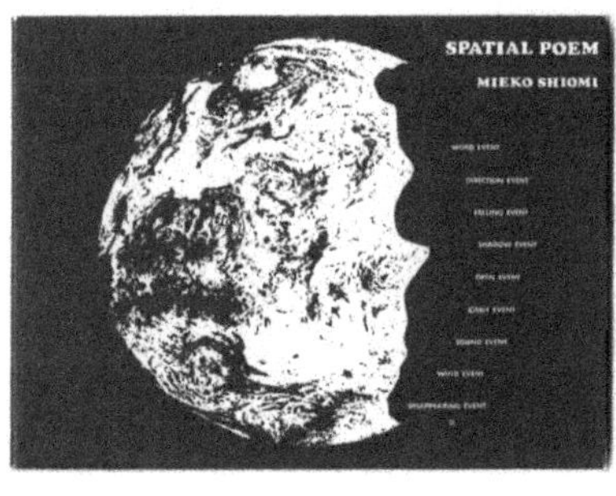

them out loud. The thing is, it's not just the poems labelled "sound poems" that were meant to be performed; Niikuni makes it crystal clear in his preface that ALL of his poems, including the "visual" ones, had a musical and oral logic to them and were meant to be read aloud. In this way, we can see that "Visual Poetry" doesn't exclude the vocal, musical, and other sonic dimensions of poetry, but is rather *even more* intimately associated with them—many of these visual poems were meant to double as springboards for experiments in new forms of poetry reading, giving the performer far more freedom in interpreting what was on the page. Keeping this in mind, "graphic scores"—experiments in alternative forms of musical notation, rejecting notes and staves for a thousand other visual formations to sing or play to—are close kin to visual poems, and also blossomed in Japan in the 1960s, with some of the most famous graphic scores worldwide being created by composers like Takemitsu Tōru, Ichiyanagi Toshi, Yuasa Jōji, and Mayuzumi Toshirō. Put yet another way: for the visual poetry in this collection, their printed existence is just the beginning. Try reading them aloud; singing them; or even better, breaking out your guitar or theremin.

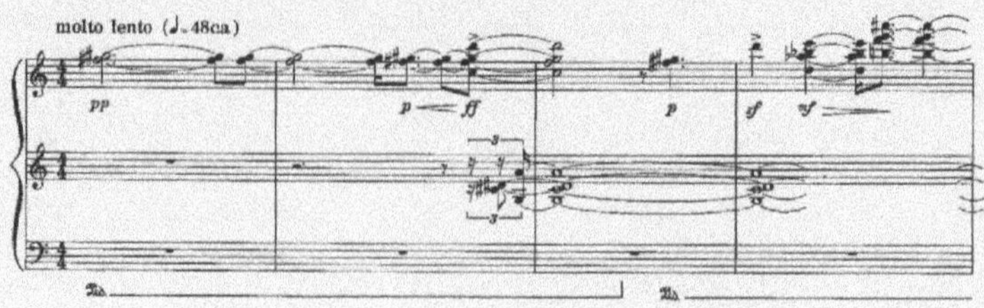

It was not a coincidence that experiments in concrete poetry like Niikuni's and other kinds of visual and intermedial poetics became so prominent across the world—especially in Brazil, Japan, Canada, and Western Europe—in the wake of World War II. These poets made their intentions clear in manifesto after manifesto: concrete poems were a way for them to attempt to knit the world together. It let them create works that were both of their language and not; that could be read across the globe without translation or with only very minor word glosses; and that could break down the boundaries between media and disciplines, remnants of a previous world regime that had only led to horror and atrocity. Niikuni and the other poets in the ASA (Association for Study of Arts) group were in constant correspondence and collaboration with other concrete and visual poets across the globe; their works became part of printed collections and gallery exhibitions spanning just about every continent. Their message hasn't lost its resonance—or its radical edge—today: break poetry out of national boundaries, including linguistic nationalism. Let it connect us. Let this most obviously-mediated kind of poetry paradoxically turn into a kind of immediacy, where to gaze on a poem is enough to achieve some level of understanding that can happen simultaneously through and beyond language, and thus bring us together. These poets were reacting to the horrors of the war; in a time like now, so characterized by vast political divisions, cruelty, and pandemic-era isolation, the goals of the concrete poets only feel more meaningful.

Another story represented here is a digital one. The spread of personal computers, of course, led to not just new kinds of visual poetry, but a new re-emphasis on the visuality of poetry more generally. Poets in Japan embraced the internet early and in great numbers, starting in the 1990s, with some experiments like the "Efu Poemu" poetry forum on NIFTY-Serve even beginning in the 1980s. For many poets, the internet was mainly

top: musical score by Jōji Yuasa

a place to upload and share their work to a different, or at least bigger audience; many did their best to recreate a conventional printed page on screen, rendering their poems in black text on a white background. Others experimented, at least, with the colors; each branch of their personal poetry pages might have a different hue—dark purple text on a sage green backdrop here, red text glaring out of the blackness there. Yet a handful took it even farther—gloriously, weirdly, and entertainingly exploring the potential of online spaces to create all new kinds of visual poetry, and even multimedia poetry.

We see these early computer-enabled practices continue to resonate into the works of many contemporary visual poets. The poet and digital artist ni_ka spent much of the 2010s creating astonishing "monitor poems" (*monita-shi*) and "Augmented Reality poems" (*AR-shi*). She declared them to be a new kind of concrete poetry, equally inspired by avant-garde poets like Niikuni and Fujitomi, as well as the radical writing practices of middle-school and teenage girls online and on their phones, who throughout the 90s and 2000s created their own kinds of visual poems through extensive use of colors, animated GIFs, emoji, kaomoji, and decomoji, but who were largely not recognized for being the radical poetic experimentalists they were. We see many other poets use the capabilities of the computer in ways that go beyond simple layout tweaks or processing tricks. In a way, the work of a computer is supposed to be invisible in conventional publishing. You're not meant to think about the Word or InDesign document that preceded the words you read on the page. Here, though, both process and outcome are made into something spectacular, as you'll see in many works in these pages.

It is difficult to capture just how thrilling this collection is to me; how refreshing, and how urgent it feels at this particular moment. In many ways, it's a wonderful time for global poetic collaborations; new groups, organization, and events constantly pop up across Japan with members from all over the world. There have never been so many translations of Japanese works coming out so quickly, too. Yet publishers—both in print and digital—face constraints in terms of budget, the logistics of printing and layout, and perceived audience interest. I am so

grateful that Taylor Mignon—a vibrant community-maker and multi-
talented poet and translator—put his formidable powers towards putting
a spotlight on both historical and contemporary works of visual poetry.
These are works that so often get left out from conversations and genealo-
gies of poetry, both in the past and in the present, so to have so many (and
so many kinds) all in one volume is an enormously valuable resource for
poets, poetry lovers, students, teachers, and scholars.

Most of all, these works do something I see as the most valuable thing
poetry can do: they invite you to make poems of your own. It's impossible
to read through these and not be inspired with ideas for creating visual
poems. They also seem to linger with you and reshape your experience
of the world; soon enough, you start to see visual poetry everywhere.
Every arrangement of paper and objects on a table, every landscape, every
jumble of advertisements, become visual poems of their own accord.
More than any other kind of poem, these works lend themselves to a
poeticization of experience, where *everything* can become part of a composi-
tion, lending even the most mundane objects expressive power, heft, and
communicative force. They show us how poetry can become something
not cordoned off, but can in fact reshape the world and the lives we live
within it.

Andrew Campana
Assistant Professor of Japanese Literature
Cornell University
Ithaca, New York, United States
November 3rd, 2023

HAIKU

upon withered bough
a crow has come to its rest…
autumnal twilight

Matsuo Bashō, haiku, 1689
Morikawa, painting
Adam Kern, translation, 2018

a winter crow
steps forward
the scene steps with him

Nagata Koi, haiku, 1930-1938
Margaret Mitsutani & Naruto Nana, translation, 2000

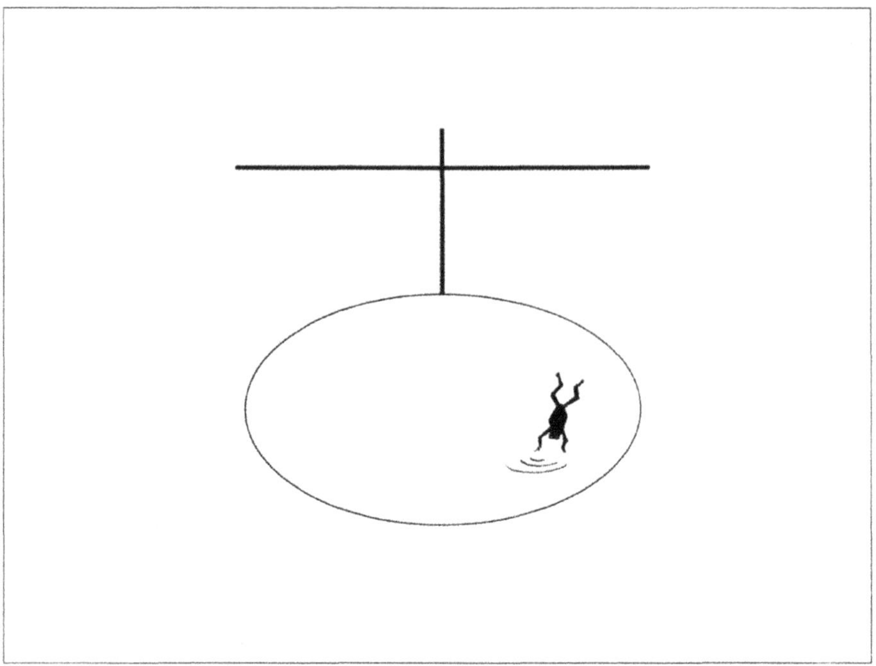

藤富　保男　水の音　　　　　　　　　　　FUJITOMI yasuo　the sound of water　1999

水の音 (mizu no oto / the sound of water)
Fujitomi Yasuo, visual translation, 1999

old pond!
a frog plunges into
watersound

Matsuo Bashō, haiku, 1681–1684
Adam Kern, translator, 2018

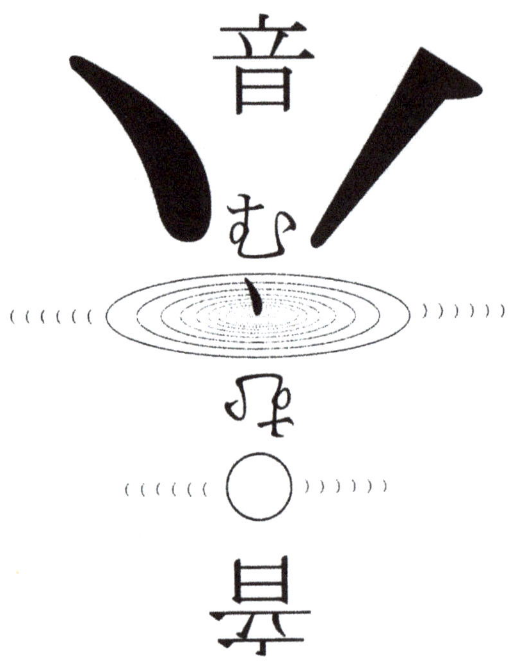

音影 (Oto kage / Sound shadow)
Yoshizawa Shoji, 2003

faraway mountains
registered in its eye
dragonfly!

Kobayashi Issa, haiku, 1763–1827
Adam Kern, translation, 2018

A machine gun —
in the middle of the forehead
a red flower blooms

Saitō Sanki, haiku, 1940
Masaya Saito, translation, 1993

A red
thread

on /
at

the no
stage.

Cid Corman, short poem, 1990

The wind
Undecided
Rolls a cigarette of air

Paul Éluard, haiku, 1920
Gilbert Bowen, translation, 1988

MODERNISM:
TAISHŌ

MANIFESTO OF THE JAPANESE FUTURIST MOVEMENT
Tokyo === HIRATO RENKICHI

MOUVEMENT FUTURISTE JAPONAIS
Par R——HYRATO

Trembling heart of the gods, the central active energy of humanity emerges from the core of collective life. The city is a motor. Its core is *dynamo-electric*.

The gods' possessions have been conquered by the arms of humans, and what was once the gods' power generator has today become the city's motor, participating in the functioning of the humanity of millions.

The instinct of the gods has been transferred to the city, and the city's dynamo-electric has jolted and awakened humanity's fundamental instinct, and has appealed to that power that attempts to push forward directly and vigorously.

The control formerly possessed by the gods has moved and become the organic relations of all life, and here dark animal fate, that stagnated discord, is beckoned out of its subservient condition; the straightforward mechanical disposition becomes a brilliant light, becomes heat, becomes constant rhythm.

MARINETTI — <*Après le règne animal, voici le règne méconique qui commence.*>

We are in the midst of a powerful light and heat. We are the children of this powerful light and heat. We are ourselves this powerful light and heat.

Intuition should be substituted for knowledge; the enemy of Futurism's anti-art is the concept. "Time and space have already died, and we already live in the absolute." We must quickly volunteer ourselves, dash forward blindly, and create. All that remains is simply the active energy of humanness that attempts to feel directly a supreme rhythm (god's instinct) in the chaos before one's eyes.

Most graveyards are already unnecessary. Libraries, art museums, and academies are not worth the noise of one car gliding down the street. As a test, try sniffing the abominable stench behind the piles of books — how many times superior is the fresh scent of gasoline!

Manifesto of the Japanese Futurist Movement
Renkichi Hirato, 1921
Miryam Sas, translation, 2004
First printed in *Cabinet* no. 13 (Spring 2004)

Futurist poets sing the praises of the many engines of civilization. These enter directly into the internal growth of the latent movement of the future, and sink deeply into a more mechanical and rapid will; they stimulate our unceasing creation, and mediate the speed and light and heat and power.

"The chameleon of dancing truth" ══ multicolored — composite — a diatonic scale of light seen in the boisterous dance of a kaleidoscope.

We, who like to be instantaneous and quick on our feet, are much indebted to Marinetti, who loved the bewitching  changes of the cinematograph; we adopt onomatopoeia, of course, and mathematical symbols, and all possible organic methods to try to participate in the essence of creation. As much as possible, we destroy the *conventions* of diction and syntax, and most of all we dispose of the corpses of adjectives and adverbs; using the infinitive mood of verbs, we advance to unconquerable regions.

There is nothing in futurism that deals in flesh — freedom of the machine — generosity — direct movement ══ only the value of absolute power's absolute.

WISH-TOYS

Fermentation......brrrr, boura, biyurrra, babiyurrrr, biyurrr...... the small explosion of a basic element that can't be seen. Felt in her ⁣　⁣, the itchy clamor of tomorrow. The unknown brilliance of the alchemist, bbbau....byuxxxx = tens of thousands boiling over in my head.

City of Tokyo enveloped in the stench of hospitals. Like the Holy mother who prays for the red jewel-colored setting sun above you, I pray for roads of good asphalt. I pray for the music of the citizens walking. City of Tokyo covered over with roses, for the brightness of stars, to people...

Girl with a diseased eye man wrapped in a bandage phosphorescent stolen child tuberculosis beriberi drippy nose weakling college student — specimen of a nervous breakdown — the feebleness of you and women, powerless to resist —kikku, kukkokku, keekku, kerokku, hiyara, vuvuvuvuvuvu, fuyangihiyaXXXXhu — ha — hu — ha — hu — ha —

— hu — haXXXXXXXXvorura, vuwibonda, borurura, do, dodo — dodo — doni — doni, vavau — vavya, vyau — vurara — rararararararara — dodo — doni ══ automobile ══ seeing off facefacefacefacefaceXXXX an invalid's fear and shuddering.

city city city city city city city city city——

people people people people people people people people——

get sick.

Automobile — sidewalk doctor — passing glint of light. Orphan of originary humanity. Strong light and heat and orphan — me — my aspirations!

Decorate with a rose, muddy ditches of Tokyo — the tenement houses and old Japanese houses mildew of office buildings on the rooftops where the sun never shines — decorate all these jails of servitude the embankments the roads, decorate them with the flowers of the drops of blood of a beautiful woman, that surround the millionaire's villa.

APHRODITE! APHRODITE! Splendor of beauty, her blinding fire, go back home to the inherent nature of woman, commit suicide, you housewives who stink of rice-bran. Scatter roses, anoint yourselves with aphrodisiacs, music of the flesh — indulgence of the faint life on the surface of the skin — into the nuance of fatigue and fire, give a strong masculine breath. Nirvana of reality. Snow white, pink, cream, fauve — in the reflection of the multicolored roses, grasp the light of silver and pearl eternity.

Vanish from my sight! Sun·moon·stars and all brilliances that silhouette black human forms. Idealist Catholic priest philosopher whose manteau reverses to vermilion and velvet. If the strong light that makes you hesitate on the threshold were to come, if there were a strong strong light greater than sun, moon, stars, lamps.....Vanish from my sight!

By Hirato Renkichi
Futurist Poetry Collection

Spiral Staircase

forthcoming

●●●●●●●●●●●●●●●●●●●●●●●●●......

By Hirato Renkichi
Futurist Novel

No Day

forthcoming

Welcome to the imagination of a new era!

Tokyo Naka-Shibuya 819
Hirato Renkichi

Translation: Miryam Sas

曙の聲

BRUU-UNBB聲

〜〜〜　聲

曙＋＋聲＋光光光

曙の聲聲聲

R

BBBB聲聲聲聲聲飛行機

●●●聲●●●●●

物聲　VON　BRUN

BRUUU•UN　聲聲聲聲聲聲

●●●●聲●●●●●

B－＋＋＋＋＋聲＋＋耕す人人人人人

BN●●聲●●聲●塔●●●●●戀●人

NO●●聲＋聲＋心のなかを耕す人人

UV●●聲聲＋バベルの塔●●耕人

－●聲山谷山バベル塔踊る人

U●新聲

R●新聲　バベルの塔　ベルの聲人人

S

B新しき聲　ル●●●人人人

新聲　塔塔塔塔人人人

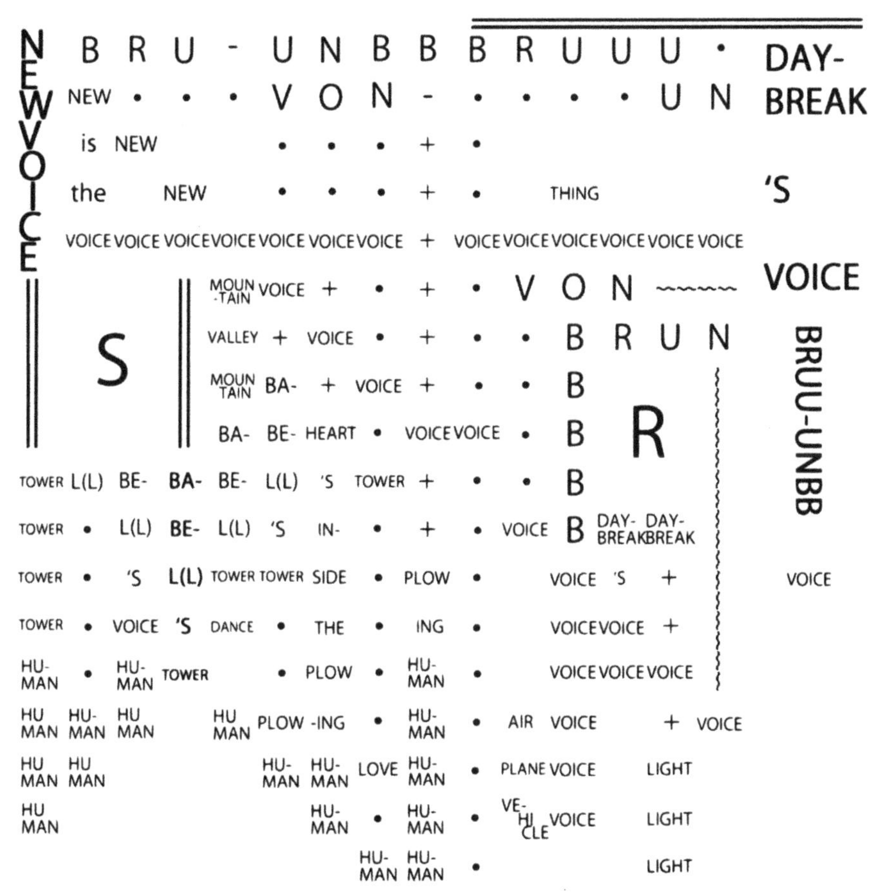

Ensemble
left: original by Renkichi Hirato, 1921 (as reproduced by R. Elizaga, 2023)
above: translation by Sho Sugita, 2017

露臺より初夏街上を見る

●　●●●　光　●

茶＝｜　花の自動車　音響　水　白光　●

コ｜＝｜　赤青　水水　水水水　光　●

ヒ｜菓＝｜　光　水煙　水光

水＝＝韮＝｜　青色　水煙　白煙●タバコS　●

髮水面足音＝　●　目　●　心臟トS　●

●女の胸顏眼＝　●　光赤〔一椅子S〕●　再　●　W光

象の鼻白白赤赤＝　●　光草S　再　●　倉庫

●耳水藥ヘヘノ＝　●　光木Z　●　再　W光汗　氷

葉耳●光光光青赤●＝　●　Z　●　再　●　汗　氷

青●エヘテナイ●＝　●　再　W光汗　氷蟲

●イヨイガキュエ●靴靴＝　○　S　再　●　馬の眼●尾

バチーン！煙●ピ×ナル光　再　W光倉庫　石炭　黒

空煙煙　煙香　●眼鏡　●足Q　赤旗　●鈴金道　●W●C

空空煙少　窓P　嶋×　●貯金　金貸　石炭

空空　皿　P　チンチンチン　PPP　緑光光

無線電信　音響　力P　空氣水沫　●チン花賣　●総光

｜立體――――｜重P　雪雪雪●　光光チン車　紫光

●●●●●●壓力PVVVラッパ●●●●チン鈴　絶望

View from a Balcony of an Early Summer Street

```
         •    —    〒 〒 〒                    x  x  x  x  x    ••••                    light    •
tea                 ‖  — flower's automobile          sound        water  white light    •
co                    ‖   — red blue • water water water water water water light    •
ffee cake              ‖   —  light           water mist         water light    •
water===pistil              ‖   —  blue color white smoke • tobacco    S    •
hair water surface footsteps ‖    •   eye  •       heart and              S    •
                                                                       car
•woman's breast face eyes        ‖    •   red light ⌠cha  ir   S    •          W          light
                                                                  car
elephant's nose white white red red ‖   •     white ⌡plant  S    •          •          warehouse
                                                             car
• ear water medicine   pistol again      ‖    •   light tree Z   •        W      light sweat ice
                                                         car
leafear • light light light blue red    •  ‖    •      Z       •    •              sweat ice
                                                    car
blue • pistol again resort               ‖      ◯        W      light sweat  ice  insect
                                                car
   •   a scream is heard      •   shoes shoes  ‖   S    •            horse's eye    •      tail
                                              car
       ding-ding!    smoke    •   pistol     light      W  light warehouse quicklime black
sky smoke smoke    smoke scent   • glasses • foot Q          red flag         gold coin    • W • C  •
sky sky smoke  surface level ————————————window P      flag  X        •  coin gold     gold coin    coal
sky sky            ⌐ L L L L L /  P        ding-ding-ding        BEEP–BEEP–BEEP      green light light
wireless          telegraph noise strength P air foam • ding flower vendor   •  green light   ∠
— solid body — — — — heavy P     snow  snow  snow • light light ding car      purple  light   ∠
•••••         pressure          P  V  V  V              horn    ••••      ding bell      despair √
```

露臺より初夏街上を見る
(View from a Balcony of an Early Summer Street)
left: original by Hagiwara Kyōjirō, 1925
above: translation by Kevin Shadel, 2018

MODERNISM:
VOU

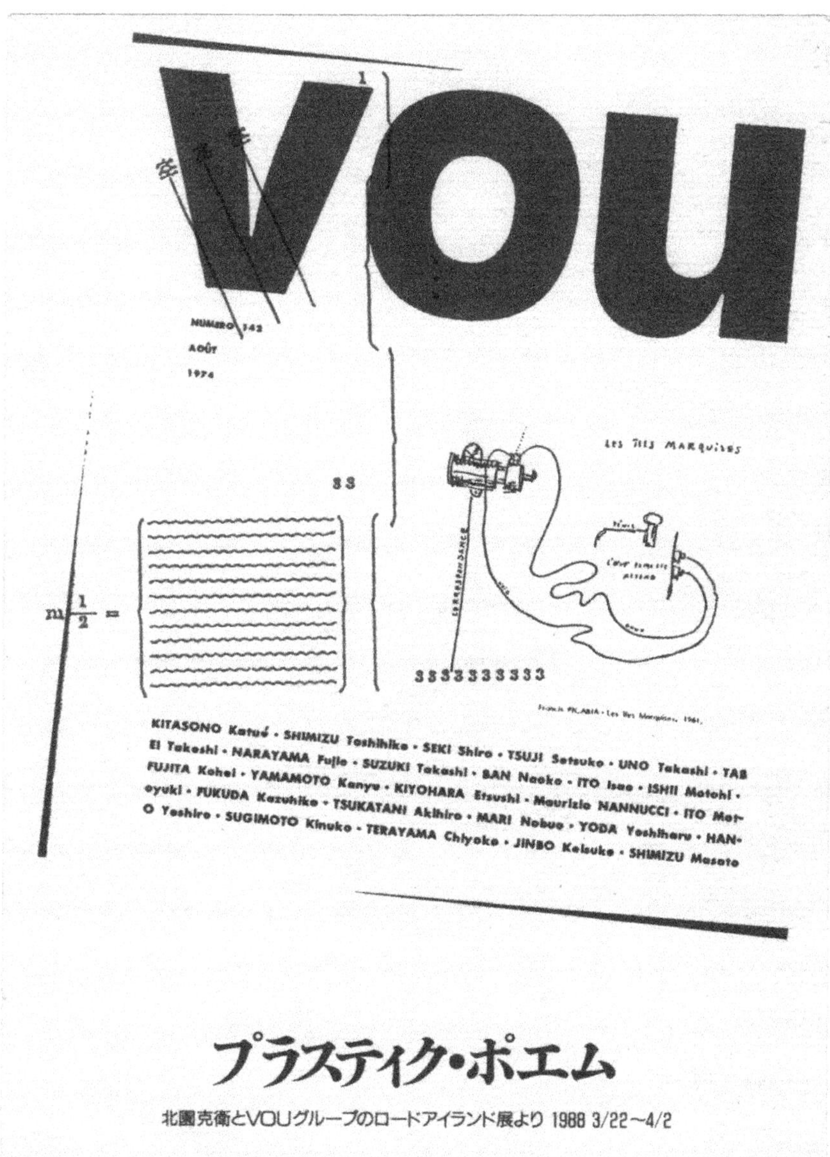

Plastic Poem
VOU exhibition postcard for Rhode Island School of Design, Yamaguchi Kenjirō, 1988

Op. 022
Tsuji Setsuko, 1969

3-minute Alpha

shoes jump off a diving board leaving footprints behind

above dusk, a bath towel falls

like needles, they stand on their heels
and have disappeared into a diagram divided into letters and numbers
a gigantic pair of tweezers descends

a journalist —operating telephoto lens —is peeping

a handkerchief
slowly stretches its wrinkles

life-sized numbers sprint at right angles

the hanky is replaced from left to right & right to left

at once the lens is blacked out

eyelashes transform into glass rods

Tsuji Setsuko, 1965
Taylor Mignon & Andrew Campana, translation, 2019

witch
Torii Ryōzen, 1977

katachi (form)
Torii Ryōzen, 1977

Kaze no gurasu (Wind's Glass)
above and top right: Torii Ryōzen, visual poem and calligram, 1957
right: Andy Houwen, translation, 2023

風のガラス

風

が キュ

カンバアの

かたちに雲を光

らすそれは緑の植物

の中の黄色い花を光らす

それは7月の村の熱いベトン

の上の太陽とガラスを黄色く光ら

すあるいは避暑地の絵ハガキの中のス

カイスクレイパアのガラスおよびその中の

無数の熱いキユカンバアの花らを黄色く光らす

Wind's Glass

W

ind   ma

kes clouds gle

am   in   cucumber

shapes it makes yellow

flowers   among   green   pla

nts gleam it makes the sun

and glass over the hot concrete of

a village in July gleam yellow or makes

the skyscraper's glass in a picture postcard and

the countless hot cucumber flowers inside gleam yellow

World in My Pocket

for example

while muttering
a merry undertaker holds his pistol

there's no mistaking
Friday the 13th

is a great day for capital punishment
right?

hey, the witch is addicted to arsenic
hey, terminate those violet pupils

on the back of a boxer standing up

a guard carved into a striped desert
and inside an elevator

a hard asparagus winter silently grows dark
my dear, what shall i give you?

Torii Shōzō, 1957 (*VOU* 91, 1963)
Taylor Mignon, translation, 2013

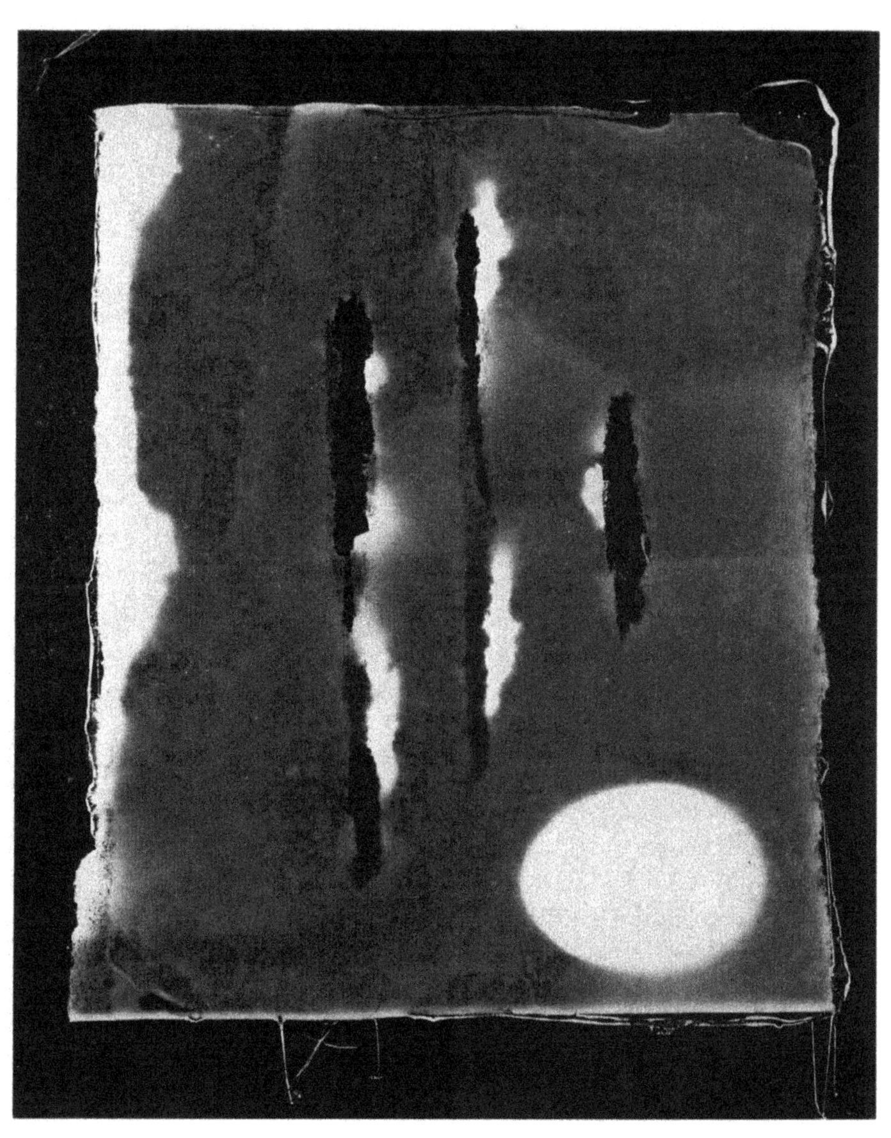

paper moon
Fukuda Kazuhiko, 1971

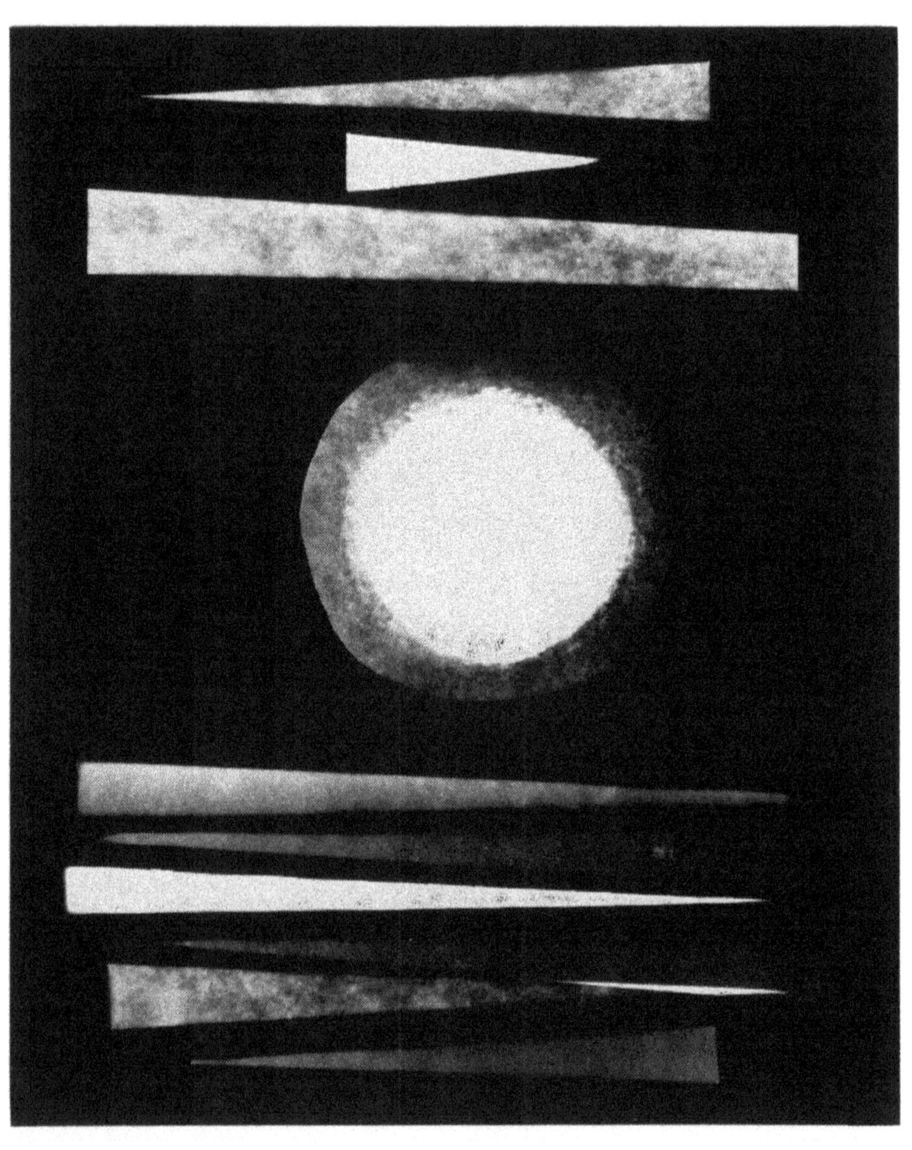

composition - op - 75
Fukuda Kazuhiko, 1975

Alfred de Vigny
Kitasono Katué

伽藍の傳説

鳥のゐない鳥籠と

鳥のゐる鳥籠がない庭から

無數の火華が立ちあがる

ヒンズウ聖徒のアポカリプスのやうに

白いコリゼの線に沿ひ

はるかにきたいなコロスをゆすぶり

夜の祭儀のサインを送る

コリブリのやうに身をくねらせて

頬づえをつく異教徒の指に

それは激しひ痺れをあたへる

Legend of a Buddhist Temple

From a birdcage without a bird

And a garden without a birdcage with a bird

Rises countless sparks

Like a Hindu apocalypse

It shakes the infinitely strange chorus

Along the lines of a white colosseum

And sends a sign for a nighttime ritual

It twists its body like a hummingbird

And gives a sharp shock

To the finger of a heathen who holds his chin in his hands

Yamamoto Kansuke, poem, *Wide Angle 2*, 1940
John Solt, translation, 1999

Buddhist Temple's Birdcage
Yamamoto Kansuke, 1940

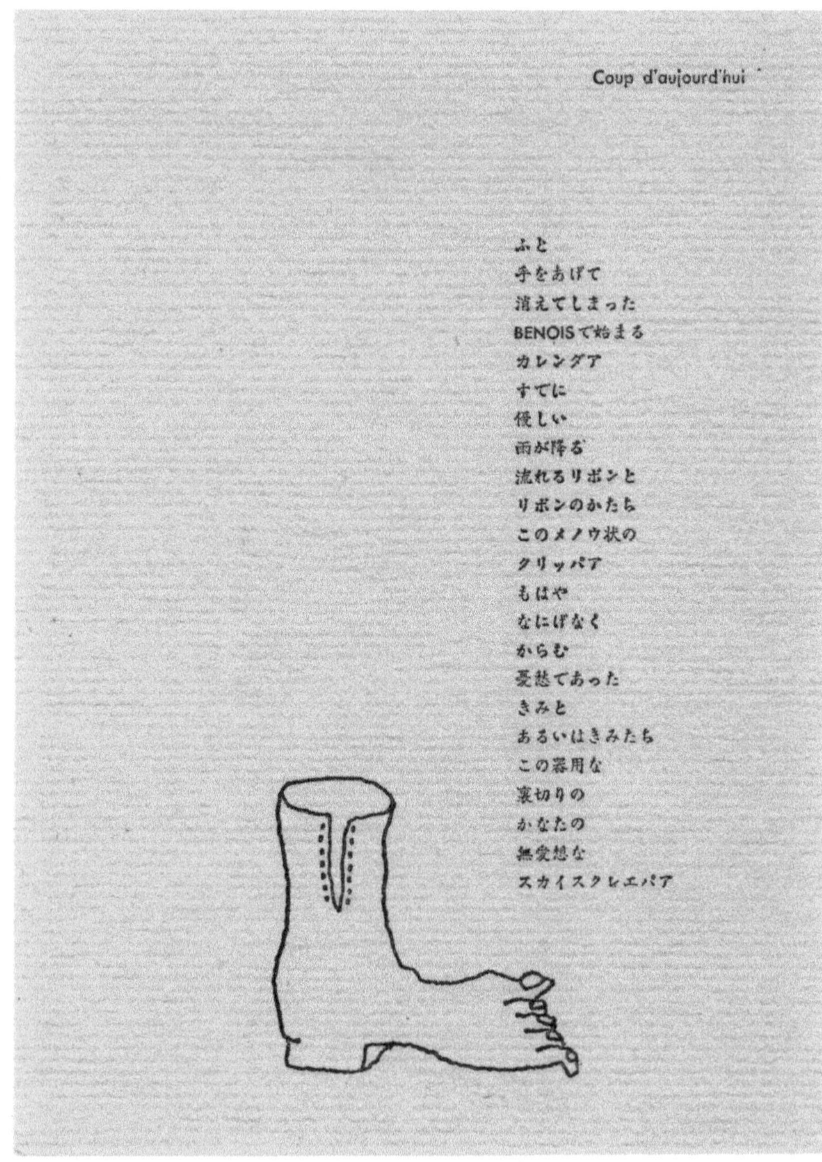

Coup d'aujourd'hui
above: Yamamoto Kansuke, *VOU*, 1959
right: John Solt, translation, 1999

Coup d'aujourd'hui

unintentionally
raising a hand
it disappeared
a calendar
starting with Benois
already
a soft
rain falls
a flowing ribbon and
a ribbon shape
this agate state's
clipper ship
already there was
casually
entangled
melancholy
you and
or you in plural
this dexterous
betrayal's
far off
surly
skyscraper

Under rose flowers of exploding black gunpowder
Girl flutters her braided hair running to the plaza
Dawn laughs out loud swaying its shoulders
Yamamoto Kansuke, 1983 (from Garcia Lorca's "Gypsy Poems")

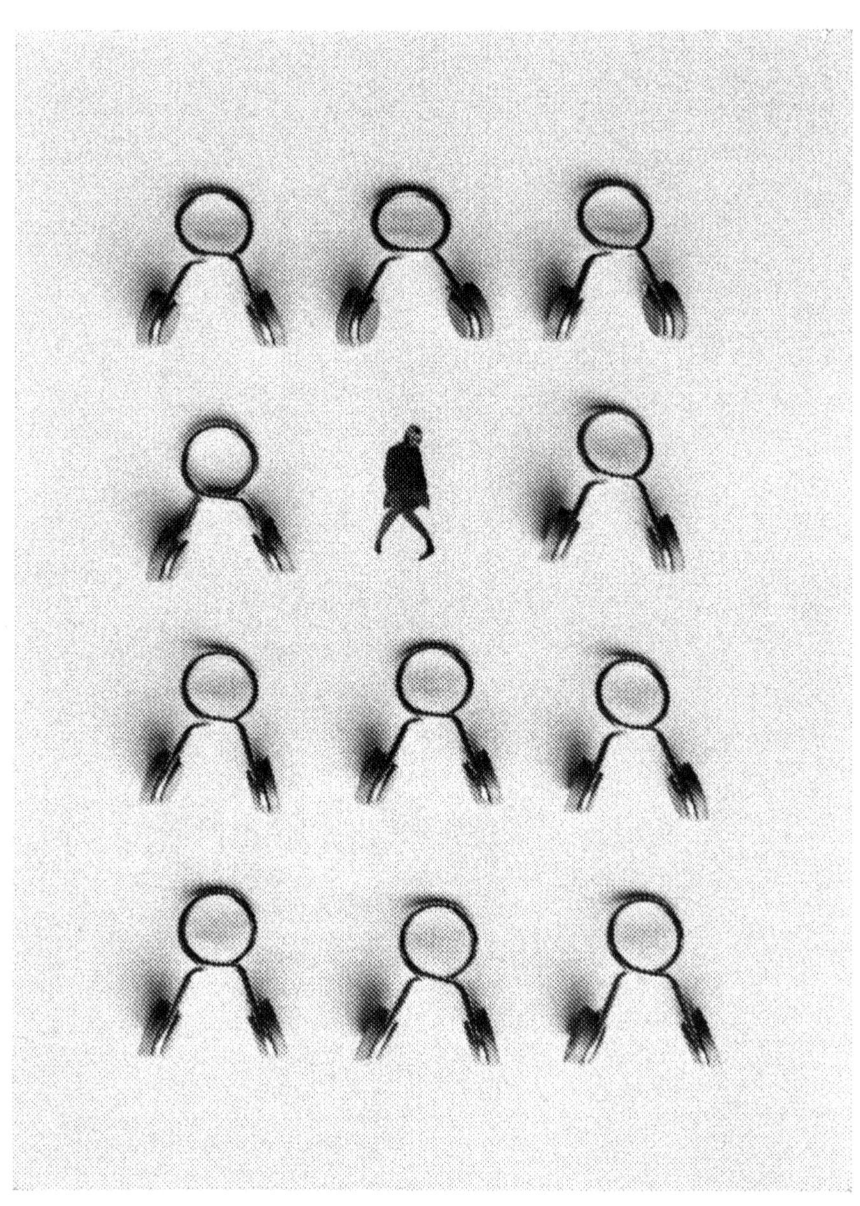

Op. 021
Tsuji Setsuko, 1969

EPHEMERA

Self-portrait with the *New York Times*
Fujitomi Yasuo, undated

SEIICHI NIIKUNI'S "RAIN"

BY KARL KEMPTON

A single moment or work luring me into visual poetics or inspiring me to compose visual poetry is not to be found. There is no point from which a single line can be drawn, except maybe from my indictable creative center. I suspect this center is but a jumble of energetic points mimicking a formed constellation of intent rooted in the more allusive intuitive from whose guiding hands I await delivery of the next gift. Perhaps this is why I view lineage as a twig in the tree of visual text art history, especially now that my studies have greatly expanded my understanding during the last two years as I write anew on the subject matter.

Seiichi Niikuni is the individual of singular import during my introductory phase to concrete poetry. Selecting an individual work of his or even his body of like work as the point or points from which to draw a line for my lineage, as the question seems to have been framed, is nebulous. His available few poems at the time formed a challenge to try to equal, having found most concrete poetry uninspiring in the Williams' *An Anthology of Concrete Poetry* and later, Solt's *Concrete Poetry*. When I thought I had perhaps accomplished my goal, it was after three or four years of dedicated effort. To this day, I hold his book, sent as a review copy by his widow, as one of my archive's treasures. Before discussing his work, I suggest a larger context triggered his influence.

I began graduate studies in economic history emphasizing in Middle Eastern studies in 1971 at the University of Utah. In the U's library was the Middle Eastern Library where I spent hours, part of which were "off course," absorbing Islamic calligraphy and art that I had quickly come to love. That was the year I diagnosed myself with dyslexia. My form is visual (reversing letters, numbers, and syllables and dropping or adding letters in words) and auditory (inability to sound out unfamiliar polysyllabic

雨 rain
Niikuni Seiichi, 1966

words along with the dropping or adding or reversing letters or syllables).
I gradually accepted its constraints and embraced its gifts, such as the ability to mentally navigate three- and four-dimensional space, see poems in words and colors vibrating off black and white patterns. If the intuitive visual flash, a "seeing" of an "incoming" poem, is part of my dyslexia or not remains unanswerable. During this period, I met Charles Potts, who was then demanding an American phonetic spelling, which solved my spelling troubles. The phoneticism accelerated my word-poem work; I soon called my word-breaking poems fissions.

Two earlier incidents, 1965 and 1966, come to mind before seeing and reading the Williams' anthology. Before being drafted into the army and then sent to Stuttgart, Germany, I heard Ken Nordine's first *Word Jazz* album. I "saw" the letters and numbers about which his marvels spun, my first such experience. The 1966 incident in Stuttgart remains with me to this day. Often I went off base into Stuttgart. My wanderings lead me to a cellar club frequented by the youth, Club Voltaire. Then, the name had no association with dada. As I descended the stairs, I noticed and took in, but uncomprehendingly, exhibited arrays of letters. While publishing *Kaldron*, upon receiving his exchange and for-review publications, I came to know that the work was concrete poems by Hansjörg Mayer.

Next to me, on my left, is an archive filing-cabinet folder full of individuals' concrete and visual poetry. The visual poem, "Rain," on display scans best from *Seiichii Niikuni: Concrete Poetry*. It is one of a handful I have been moved by because of its clarity, a presentation both simple and complex. Stare unblinkingly at it; it is an optic wonder of shimmering raindrops. Stare longer, and the rain drops through a rainbow. I understand that Crag Hill will also discuss Niikuni, his "River and Sandbank" poem. These two and a few others of like expression inexplicably attracted me. The only explanation I can now offer is the kindred spirit and patterning similar to the Arabic works informed by Persian and Byzantine patterns I was first drawn to and "eye" and "heart" trained by. Eventually, I came to know this piece had an undercurrent, a subtle unemotional and objective reference to an earlier emotional "Rain," the

"Il pleut" calligramme by Apollinaire, who is both a mistaken beginning or second point in visual text art histories and a point for many lineages disguised as histories.

We are confronted with a paradox by these two works, one based on a misunderstanding of the ideogram, the root of the calligramme, and the other unwittingly seems to support the misconception that the ideogram is pictorial, not phoenetic. Apollinaire first called his visual poems ideograms; his initial and basic understanding of the visual aspects of the ideogram was commonplace at that time among non-Chinesě speakers, and Pound's heralding its supposed pictorialness only added to the confusion among uninformed literati. It appears also that the term *calligramme* was first used by the Chiliean poet, Vicente Huidobro, and later mistakenly credited to Apollinaire (as were other terms and movements, –isms, for which there is no room to digress into). Concrete theory continued the misinterpretation of the ideogram being pictorial by demanding the replacement of lyrical language, common among the many calligramme poets who remain obscure footnotes hidden by Apollinaire's large, inflated shadow, to a highly rigid geometric patterning of language. Niikuni's "Rain" fit nicely into the theory as did other of his works. It would be as if one outside the knowledge of the European alphabets stated proof that they were pictorial because the letter "A" is an ox head, "B" a house, etc., or that ") (" are new and old moons.

Perhaps Niikuni's piece is not the unemotional, objective, geometric, concrete presentation on rain found within its kanji ideogram. Perhaps it is directly composed as an additional and deeper companion to Apollinaire's "Il pleut" as a subjective, emotional, and political visual repetitive haiku–like lyric expressing grief of, and also by, innocent victims of war. In Niikuni's work, the rain can read as the Black Rain, rain contaminated with radiation after the bombings of Hiroshima and Nagasaki. Additionally, the rain can be the torrent of tears caused by continued aftermath from these bombings.

Autumn Equinox, 2015
Oceano, CA

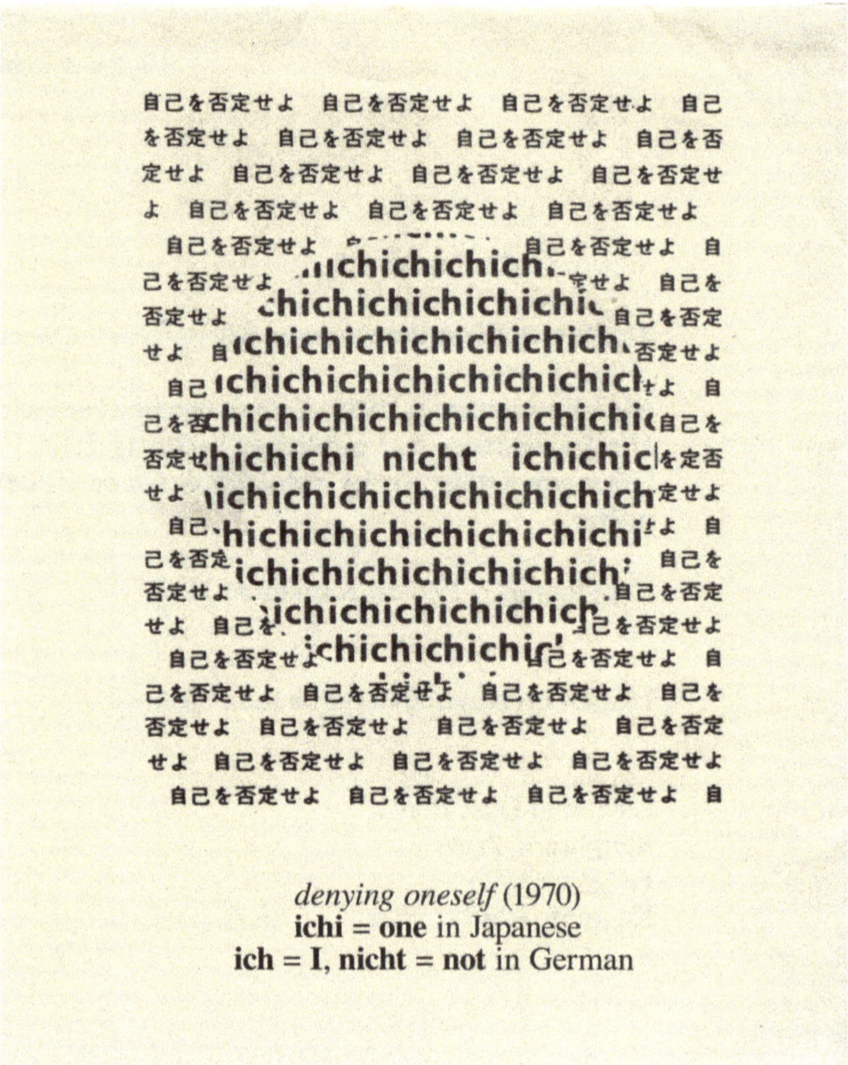

自己を否定せよ　自己を否定せよ　自己を否定せよ　自己
を否定せよ　自己を否定せよ　自己を否定せよ　自己を否
定せよ　自己を否定せよ　自己を否定せよ　自己を否定せ
よ　自己を否定せよ　自己を否定せよ　自己を否定せよ
　自己を否定せよ　　　　　　　　　　自己を否定せよ　自
己を否定せよ　　ııchichichich　　せよ　自己を
否定せよ　　chichichichichichi　自己を否定
せよ　自ıchichichichichich　否定せよ
　自ichichichichichichichi　せよ　自
己を否chichichichichichichi　自己を
否定せ hichichi nicht ichichic　定否
せよ ııchichichichichichich　定せよ
自己 hichichichichichichichi　よ　自
己を否定 ichichichichichich　自己を
否定せよ ııchichichichichich　自己を否
せよ 自己を ichichichichich　己を否定せよ
自己を否定せよ ichichichichi　己を否定せよ　自
己を否定せよ　自己を否定せよ　自己を否定せよ　自己を
否定せよ　自己を否定せよ　自己を否定せよ　自己を否
せよ　自己を否定せよ　自己を否定せよ　自己を否定せよ
　自己を否定せよ　自己を否定せよ　自己を否定せよ　自

denying oneself (1970)
ichi = one in Japanese
ich = I, nicht = not in German

denying oneself
Kamimura Hiro, 1970

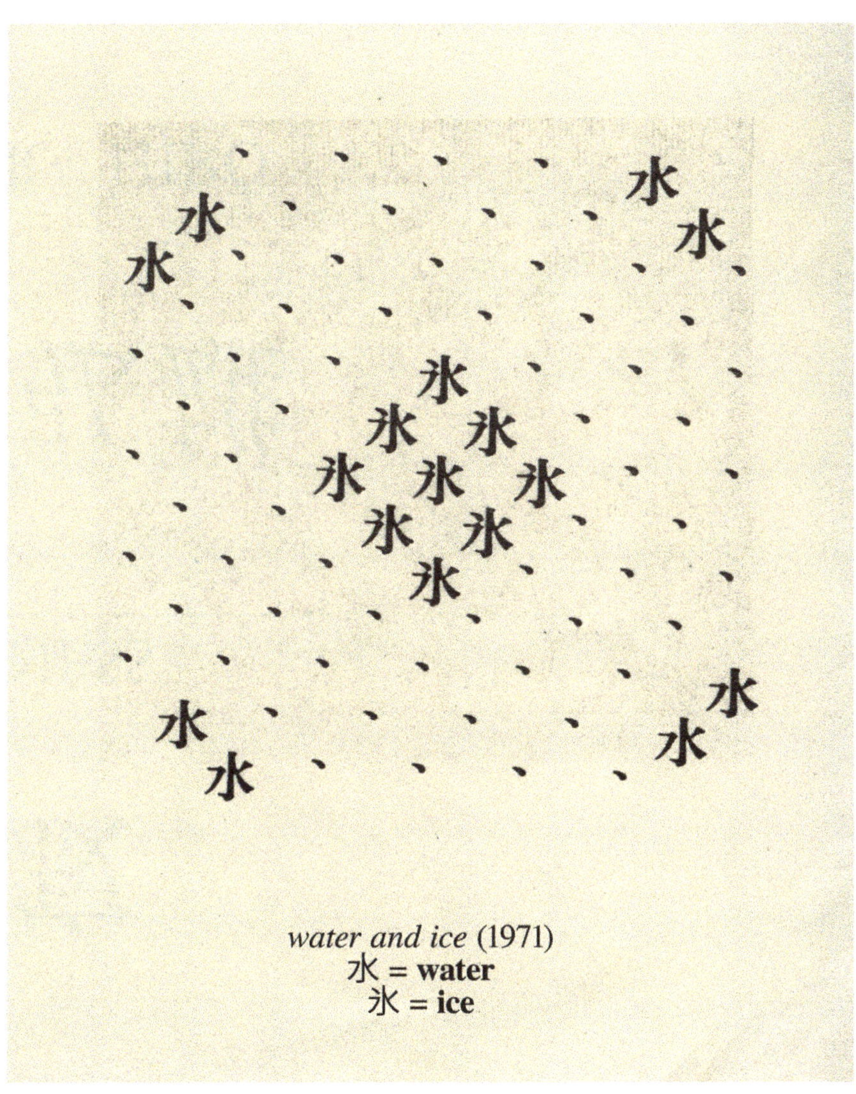

water and ice
Kamimura Hiro, 1971

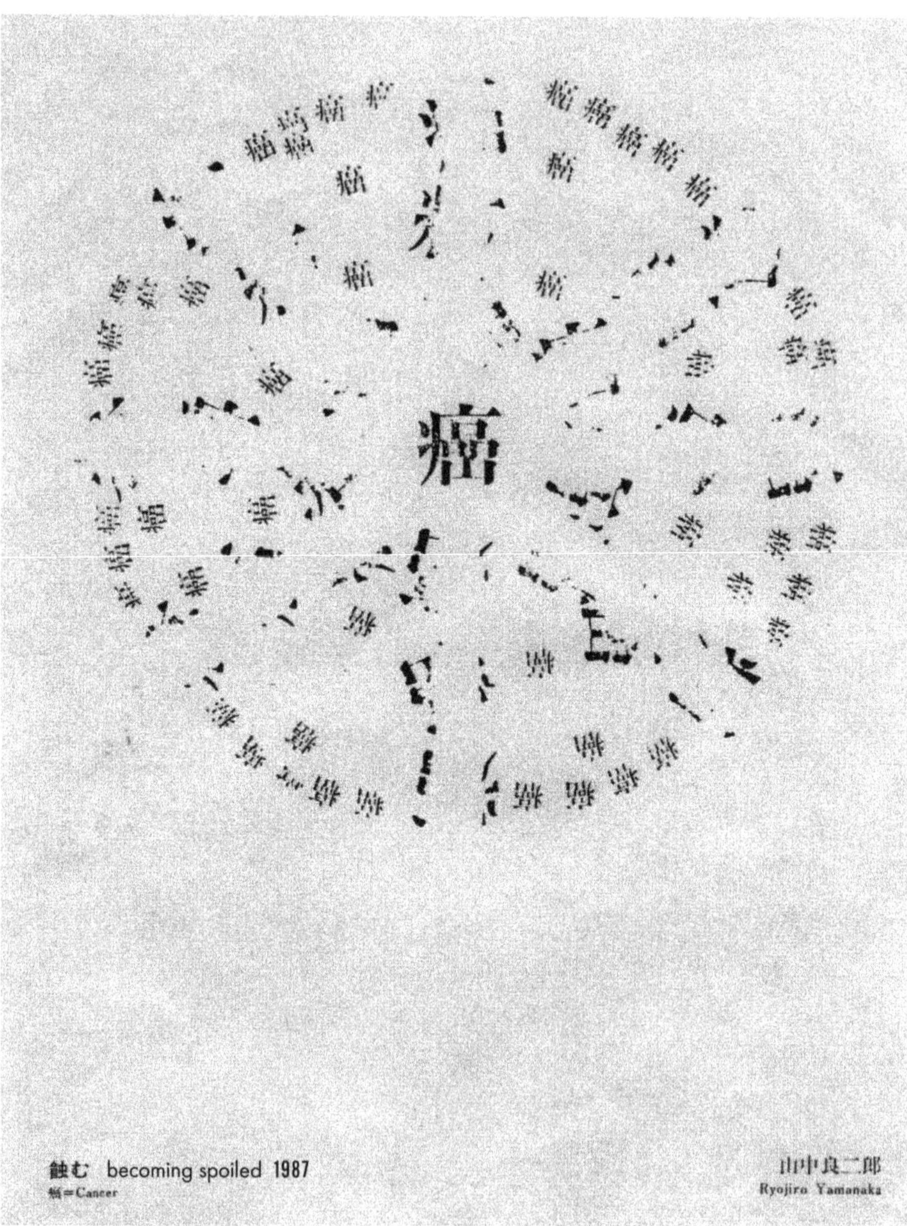

becoming spoiled
Yamanaka Ryojiro, 1987

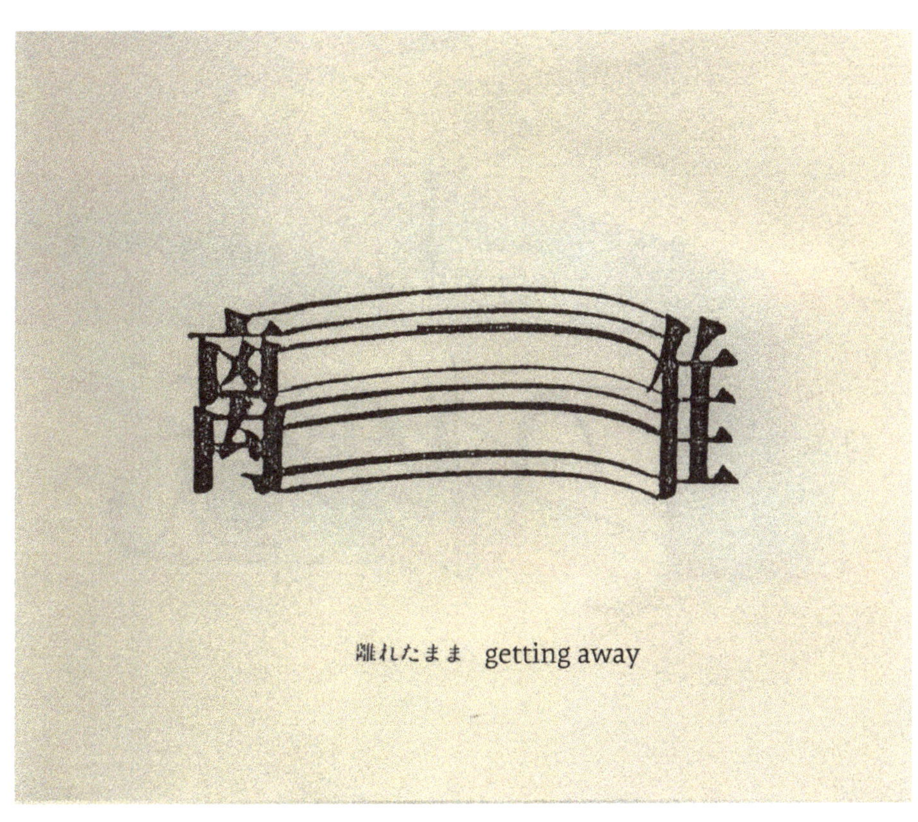

getting away
Tanabu Hiroshi, 1991

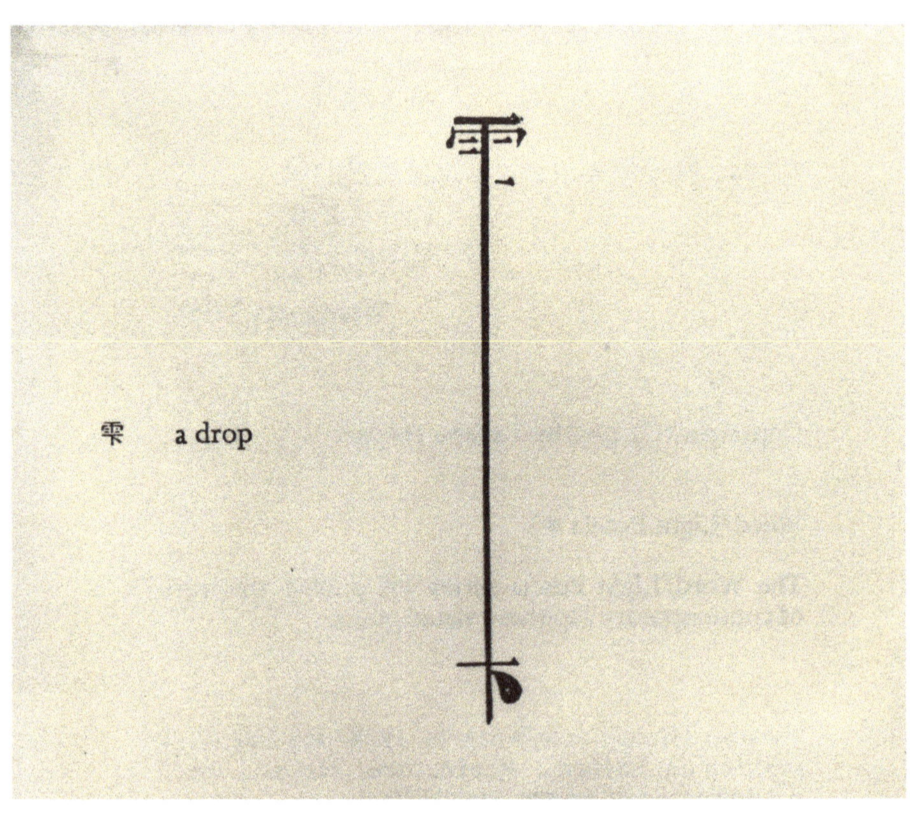

a drop
Tanabu Hiroshi, 1991

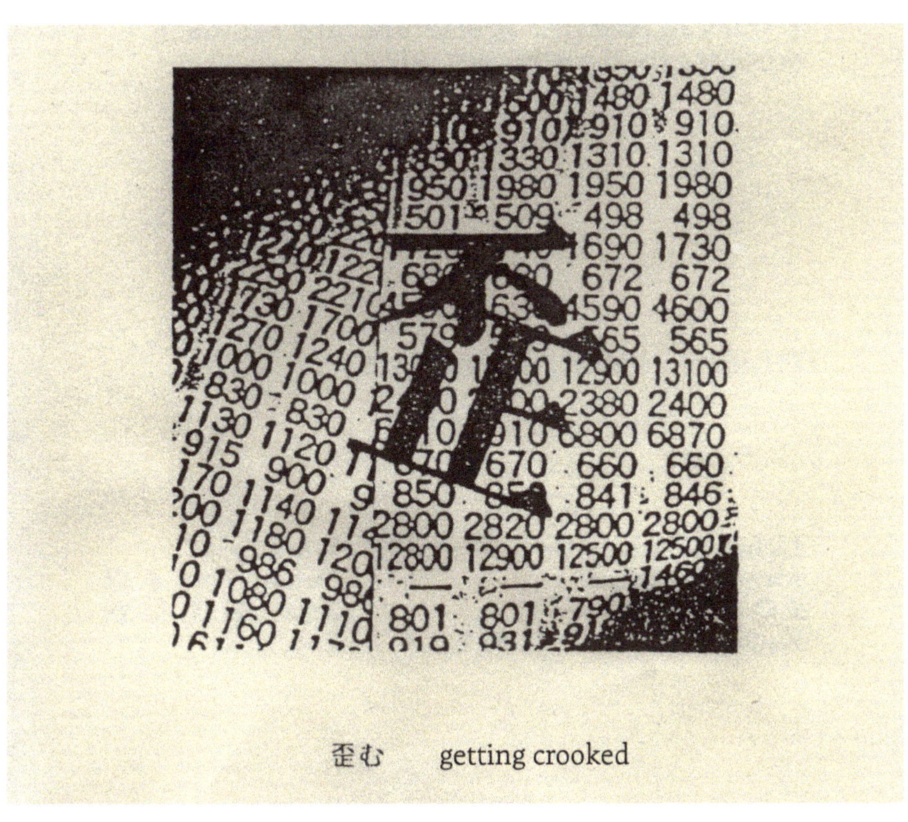

getting crooked
Tanabu Hiroshi, 1991

Hagiwara Sakutaro

words climb over words and emotions do the loop the loop
life loses its footing and the soul tumbles down
even one truth becomes wrapped in a veil of fallacy
the retina turned demented perfectly diffuses light
all words can do is reflect
yet verse make words work hard
poetry is also delusion
(Sakutaro took oblivion from delusion just
as a dream is perceived)
emotions somersault, words climb over each other
truth is made bare
phenomena coagulates
a poem is a lens
the camera obscura a vortex of light

top:
Onchi Kōshirō, portrait of Sakutaro Hagiwara (the author of *Ice Island*), 1943

above:
Onchi Kōshirō, poem, 2000; Taylor Mignon, translation

LOOKING A GIFT HORSE IN THE MOUTH

BY JOHN SOLT

When I was a graduate student, I noticed that the Harvard-Yenching Library had book exhibits in a three-shelved, dedicated space viewable from both outside and inside the library upon entering. I became friends with the librarian in charge, and he was pleased that I offered to do an exhibition series of seven Japanese book designers over two years. I chose graphic artists who had created their own signature styles, regardless of their level of fame in Japan. I figured that none of the viewers would know any of the names of the designers, so their fame was irrelevant.

I approached graphic designer Yamaguchi Kenjirō to design the direct mail postcards, one per artist. During 1989 and 1990, the exhibits were held in the following order: Onchi Kōshirō, Kitasono Katué, Sugiura Kōhei, Ohie Toshio, Takahashi Shōhachirō, Kiyohara Etsushi, and Yamaguchi Kenjirō. The postcards arrived one by one in time for each exhibit.

The back sides of the cards were identical, consisting of a list of the seven participants, and they were only distinguishable by a dot on the left side of the artist's name for each specific exhibit.

When it came time for the last one—Yamaguchi Kenjirō's own exhibit—he sent as his front side of the card the same template he had designed for the back of each of the cards. It was a humorous way to remind viewers that he had designed the whole set. Because Kenjirō was a sensitive graphic artist, he subtly changed the shades of grey and black on the front and back of his own card.

The exhibits were a success and gained attention far and wide. The British Museum took interest, received a set, and advertised the exhibits from across the pond. In 1993-94 the same seven exhibits were displayed in the same order at Amherst College in its Robert Frost Library.

I made it a point to put a photograph of the designer next to their books in each exhibit, because we rarely see designers' portraits, unlike with authors and painters.

I offered to donate to the Harvard-Yenching Library all of my books that they had exhibited, on the condition that the library would create a card catalog entry for each designer. Otherwise, the individual books would be listed as usual by author only, and the designers' names would be lost in the book colophons, remaining buried in the immense stacks and irrecoverable for eternity. Without a card catalog entry, who would be able to reassemble them or find even one designer's book?

Unfortunately, the library staff adamantly refused, insisting that there was no precedent for my request. Because they had never created a card catalog category for book designers, they weren't going to start now. Thirty-five years later the books remain uneasily perched on my bookshelves, waiting for an earthquake or another method of disposal.

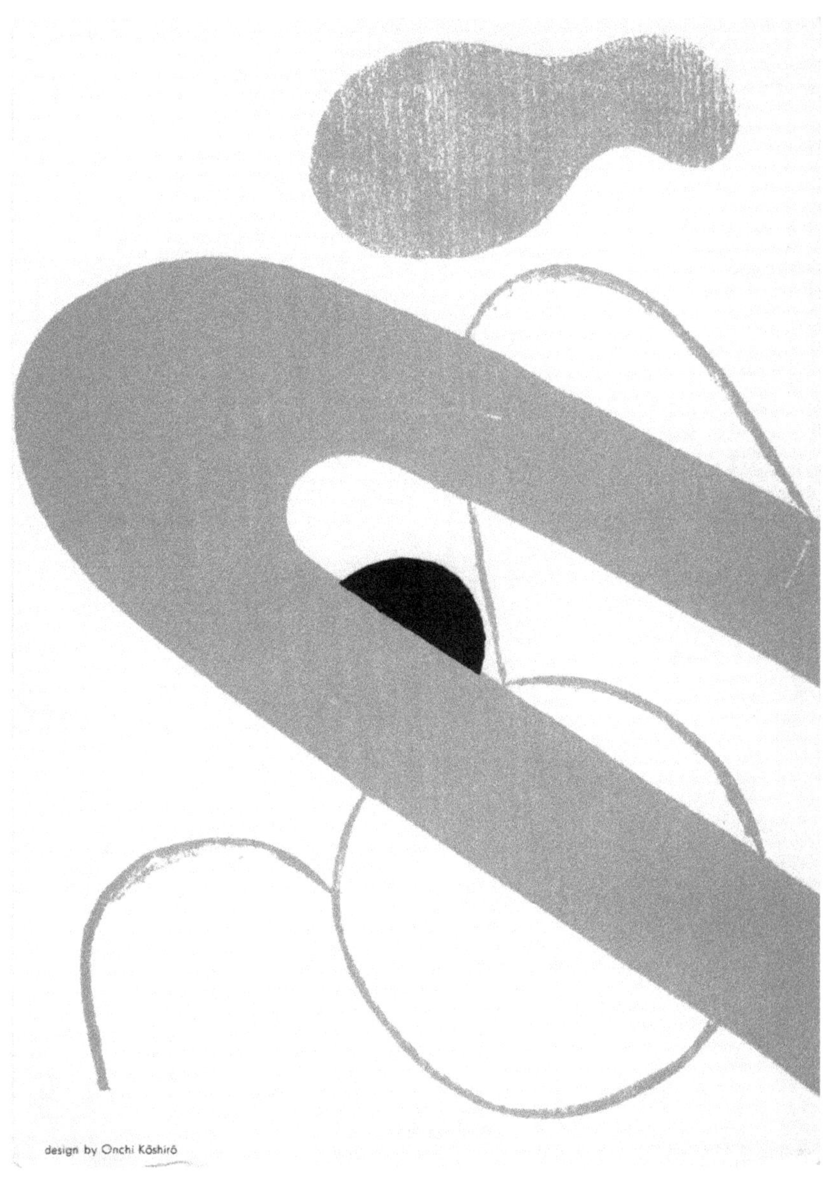

Postcard for "Japanese Avant-Garde Book Design"
Onchi Kōshirō
Promotional postcard for an exhibition series at
Harvard University, 1989–1990

Postcard for "Japanese Avant-Garde Book Design"
Kitasono Katué
Promotional postcard for an exhibition series at
Harvard University, 1989–1990

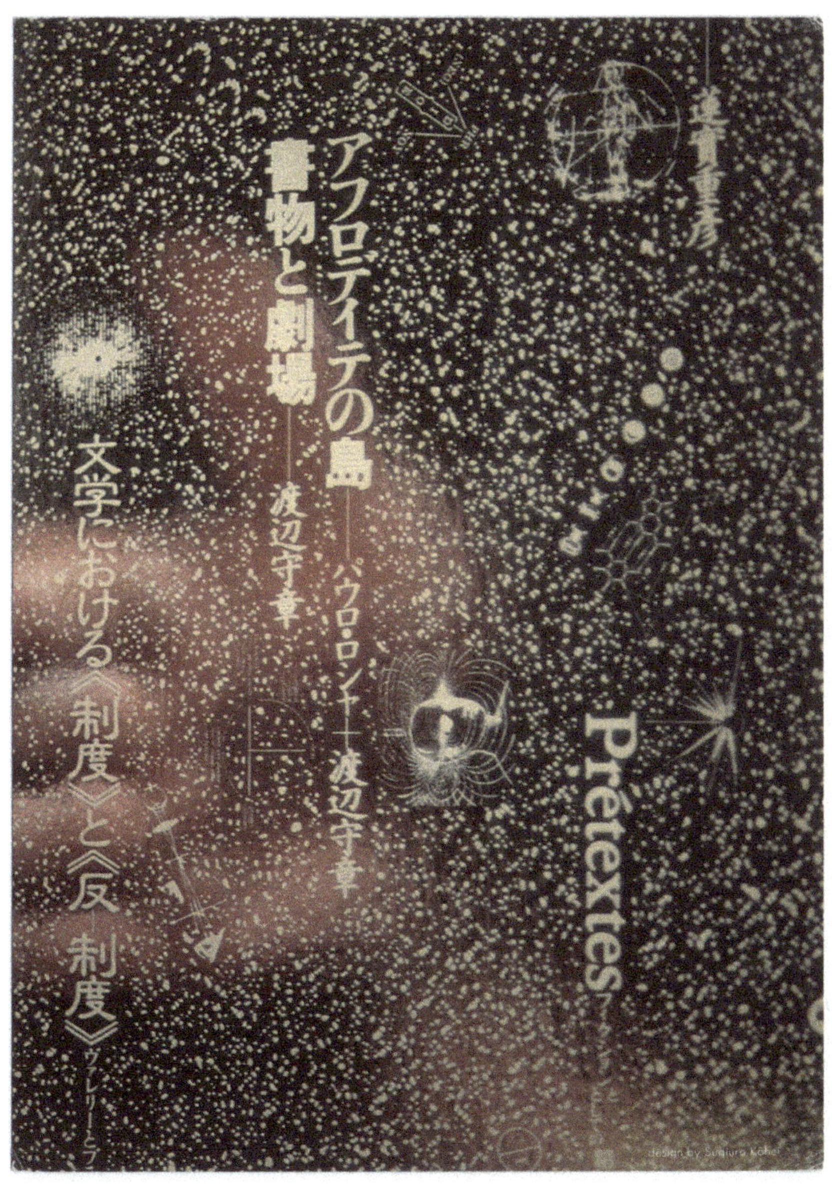

Postcard for "Japanese Avant-Garde Book Design"
Sugiura Kōhei
Promotional postcard for an exhibition series at
Harvard University, 1989–1990

Postcard for "Japanese Avant-Garde Book Design"
Ohie Toshio
Promotional postcard for an exhibition series at
Harvard University, 1989–1990

Postcard for "Japanese Avant-Garde Book Design"
Takahashi Shōhachirō
Promotional postcard for an exhibition series at
Harvard University, 1989–1990

Postcard for "Japanese Avant-Garde Book Design"
Kiyohara Etsushi
Promotional postcard for an exhibition series at
Harvard University, 1989–1990

Postcard for "Japanese Avant-Garde Book Design"
Yamaguchi Kenjirō
Promotional postcard for an exhibition series at
Harvard University, 1989–1990

EASY ENTRY: Postcard-Stamp-Text

I make collages using three elements: (1) postcard; (2) found text; (3) stamp. Postcards and stamps as commercial objects are intrinsically art from the get-go. The found texts on paper contain writing of various sizes, fonts, and colors. The mix of postcard, text, and stamp creates ricocheting perceptions.

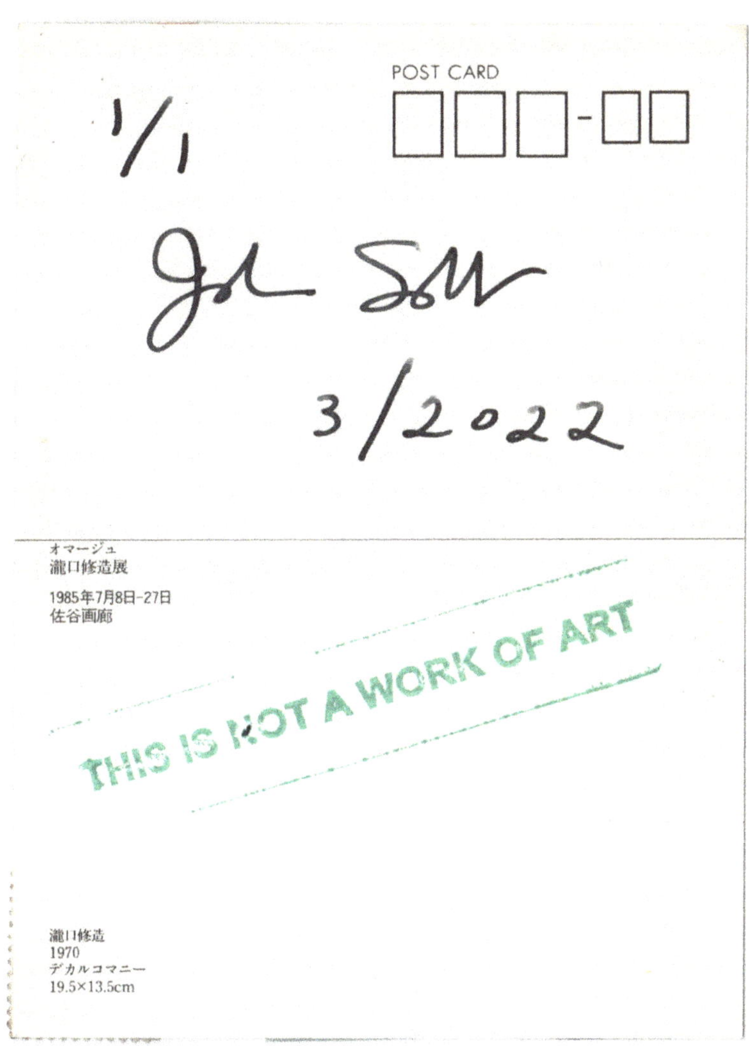

Untitled postcard collage (*left:* front, *above:* back)
John Solt, 2022

I get pleasure knowing that nothing springs directly from my head (as do my words in poetry), but in the combining and composing of the three elements there's enough of my sensibility to make the act creative, fun, and relaxing—a kind of semi-conscious automatism in which I often lose the sense of time passing.

Untitled postcard collage (*above:* front, *right:* back)
John Solt, 2021

I've done about 1,400 collages over the last dozen years. On the back of each I write (with tongue firmly in cheek): 1/1, signature, month and year, and then stamp them: "This Is Not A Work Of Art."

—John Solt

CONTEMPORARY

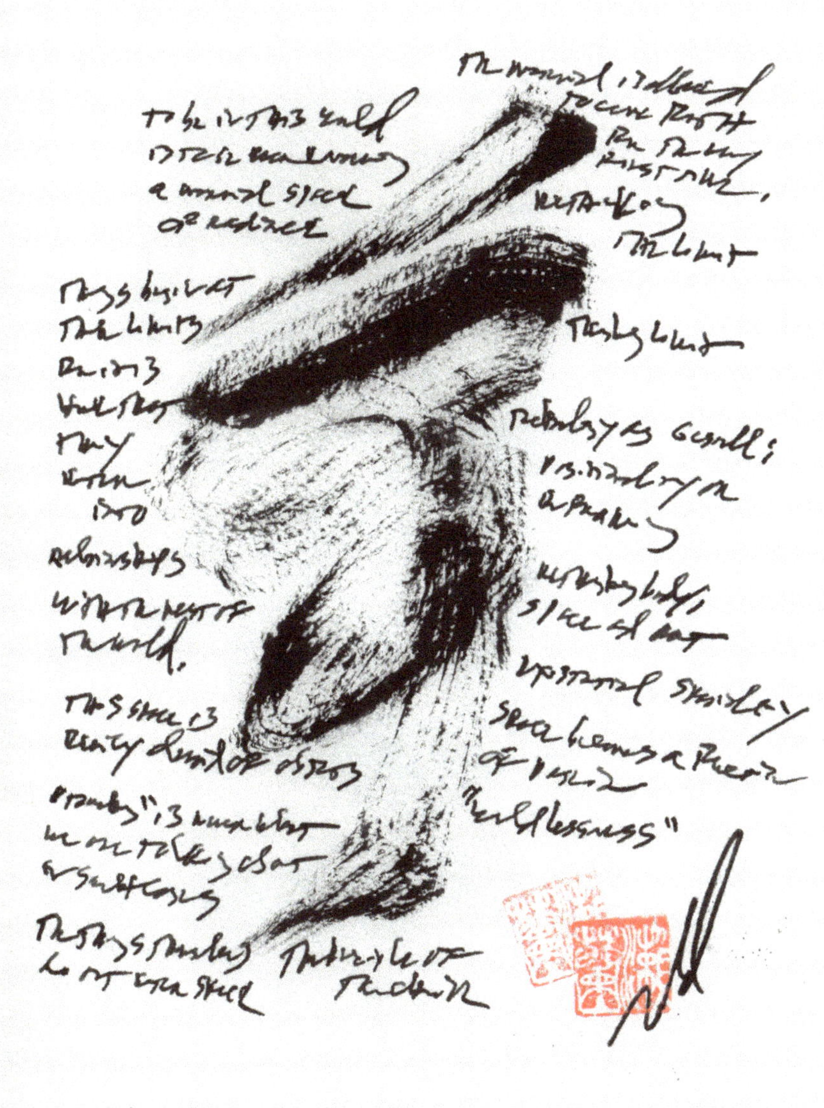

Untitled
Eric Selland, asemic calligraphy, 2022

Untitled
Eric Selland, asemic calligraphy, 2022

Untitled
Eric Selland, asemic calligraphy, 2022

above:
Ink drawing
John F. Cross

right:
Poem by Jeffrey Johnson
*"In dedication to the memory of,
and in collaboration with, Our Drunk Poets
brother-in-letters dearest, John Francis Cross."*

Determined Spirit at the Exchange

stack vertebrae
continental breakfast
collected cells
trouble in a spirited body
How? When? Why?
Whose prayers does she refuse?
a symphony
i see
in harmony
and discord
collision bound
the beauty of numbers
surrounded circularity
bounded by skin
deeply troubled within
a masked John
playful soul
as fish in water
Chaplinesque gags
underground
the sweet sewer stench
called time
Cross to bear
black crack
electric shock
the nerve
a bridge too far
too far
karmic
wheel
cannot bind
spirited manchild
Live to Laugh
Laugh to Live
turbulent trajectory
ahead
bound as we are
in
matter
in
time

For a
brief
mom
entth
eyfad
edwit
houta
waren
essdar
knessw
asupon
thedom
ain For
a brief m
oment th
eyfadedwit
houtawaren
essdarknessw
asthedomain F
or a brief mome
nt they faded with
outawarenessdarkn
esswasuponthedoma
in For a brief moment
they faded without a war

They
faded
witho
utawar
anawar
enessof
awardark
nessthedo
main They f
aded without
awareness They
fadedwithoutawa
renessofawardarkn
essthedomaintheyfad
edforabriefmomentthe
yfadedwithoutawareness
thedomainofdarknesswasto
becomethemtheyfadedintofa
ding They without awareness a
war They without awareness a
domain of darkness would be
cometheyfadedwithoutawar
enessforabriefmomentthey
theyfadedwithoutawarenes
sdarknesswasthedomain

Untitled Blue #21
Steven Karl, 2022

```
the              as      on
guts             if      ly
   of            wi      im
feel             nd      ag
ings             co      in
they             er      at
could            ce      io
     not         df      n
        feel     el      or
           but   t       th
sadness          ru      at
enough           in      in
   to            ed      be
know—            up      tw
                 on        ee
                 fa          n
                 ce          wh
                  ,            ere
```

Untitled Blue #22
Steven Karl, 2020–2021

```
TOKYOTOKYOTOKYOTOKYOTOKYOTOKYOTOKYOTOKYOTOKYOTOKYO
KYOTOKYOTOKYOTOKYOTOKYOTOKYOTOKYOTOKYOTOKYOTOKYOTO
TOKYOTOKYOTOKYOTOKYOTOKYOTOKYOTOKYOTOKYOTOKYOTOKYO
KYOTOKYOTOKYOTOKYOTOKYOTOKYOTOKYOTOKYOTOKYOTOKYOTO
TOKYOTOKYOTOKYOTOKYOTOKYOTOKYOTOKYOTOKYOTOKYOTOKYO
KYOTOKYOTOKYOTOKYOTOKYOTOKYOTOKYOTOKYOTOKYOTOKYOTO
TOKYOTOKYOTOKYOTOKYOTOKYOTOKYOTOKYOTOKYOTOKYOTOKYO
KYOTOKYOTOKYOTOKYOTOKYOTOKYOTOKYOTOKYOTOKYOTOKYOTO
TOKYOTOKYOTOKYOTOKYOTOKYOTOKYOTOKYOTOKYOTOKYOTOKYO
KYOTOKYOTOKYOTOKYOTOKYOTOKYOTOKYOTOKYOTOKYOTOKYOTO
TOKYOTOKYOTOKYOTOKYO          TOKYOTOKYOTOKYOTOKYO
KYOTOKYOTOKYOTOKYOTO          KYOTOKYOTOKYOTOKYOTO
TOKYOTOKYOTOKYOTOKYO          TOKYOTOKYOTOKYOTOKYO
KYOTOKYOTOKYOTOKYOTO          KYOTOKYOTOKYOTOKYOTO
TOKYOTOKYOTOKYOTOKYO          TOKYOTOKYOTOKYOTOKYO
KYOTOKYOTOKYOTOKYOTOKYOTOKYOTOKYOTOKYOTOKYOTOKYOTO
TOKYOTOKYOTOKYOTOKYOTOKYOTOKYOTOKYOTOKYOTOKYOTOKYO
KYOTOKYOTOKYOTOKYOTOKYOTOKYOTOKYOTOKYOTOKYOTOKYOTO
TOKYOTOKYOTOKYOTOKYOTOKYOTOKYOTOKYOTOKYOTOKYOTOKYO
KYOTOKYOTOKYOTOKYOTOKYOTOKYOTOKYOTOKYOTOKYOTOKYOTO
TOKYO      TOKYOTOKYOTOKYOTOKYOTOKYOTOKYOTOKYOTOKYO
KYOTO        KYOTOKYOTOKYOTOKYOTOKYOTOKYOTOKYOTOKYOTO
TOKYOTOKYOTOKYOTOKYOTOKYOTOKYOTOKYOTOKYOTOKYOTOKYO
KYOTOKYOTOKYOTOKYOTOKYOTOKYOTOKYOTOKYOTOKYOTOKYOTO
TOKYOTOKYOTOKYOTOKYOTOKYOTOKYOTOKYOTOKYOTOKYOTOKYO
KYOTOKYOTOKYOTOKYOTOKYOTOKYOTOKYOTOKYOTOKYOTOKYOTO
```

A Small Map of Modern Japan
Paul Rossiter, 1995

No title
Aram Saroyan, 1966

Juror Appreciation Week
Ray Craig, 2021

Untitled collage
FLANGER, 2022

Untitled collage
FLANGER, 2022

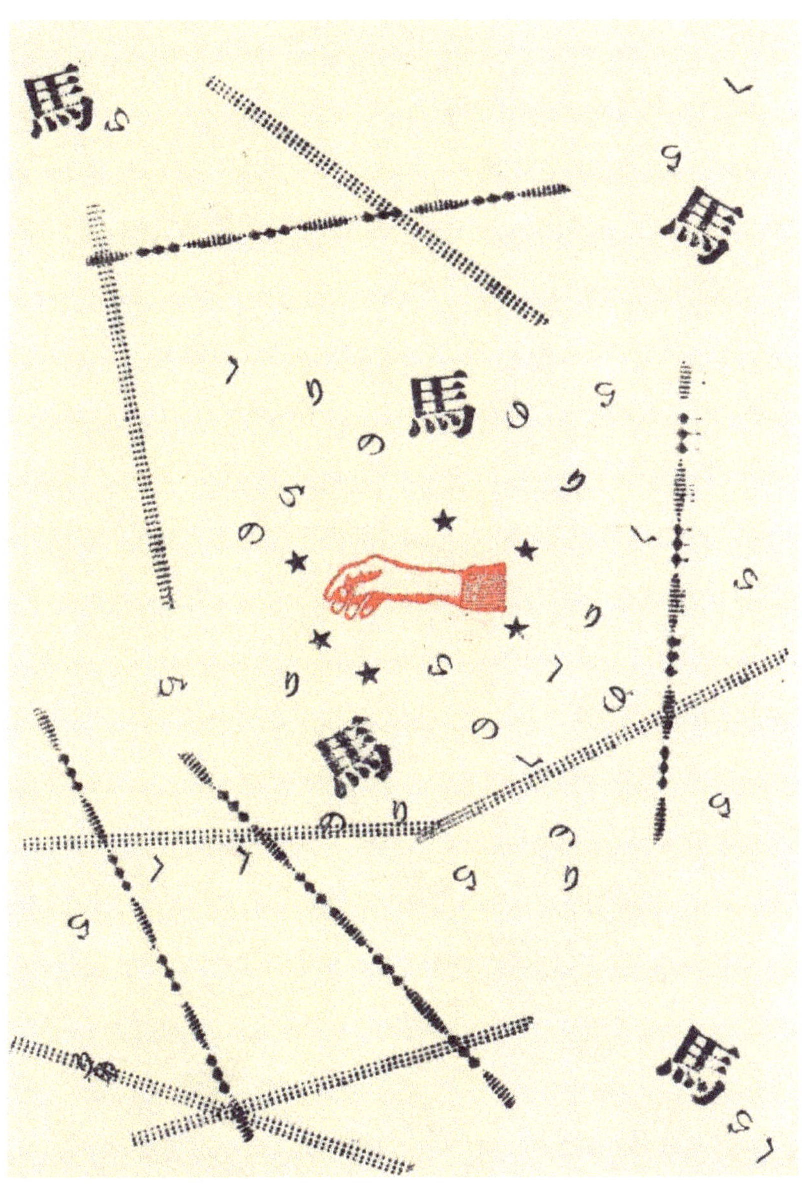

Untitled
Nakamura Keiichi, 2022

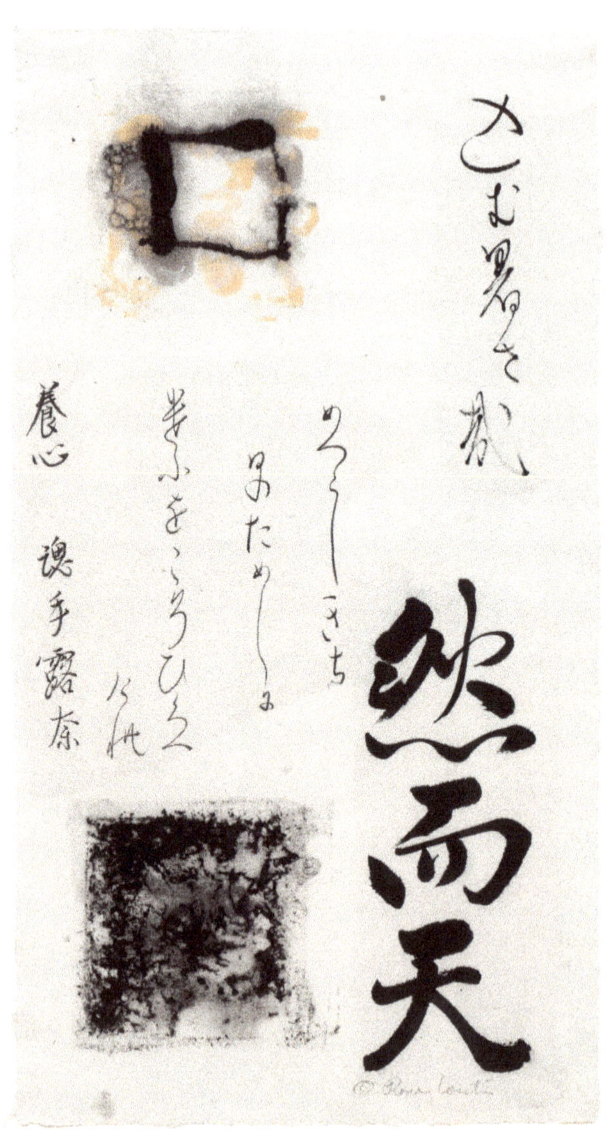

Heavenly Fields
Rona Conti, calligraphy, 2014

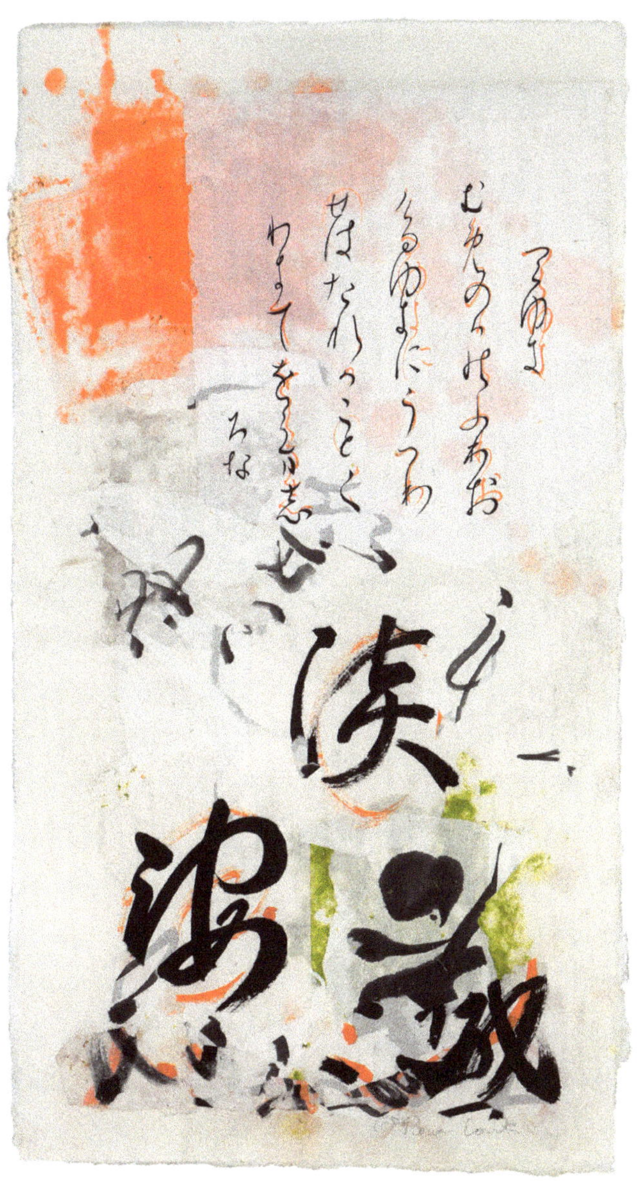

Fragments
Rona Conti, calligraphy, 2014

only murmur with blue, red and yellow
Herman Bartelen, 1999

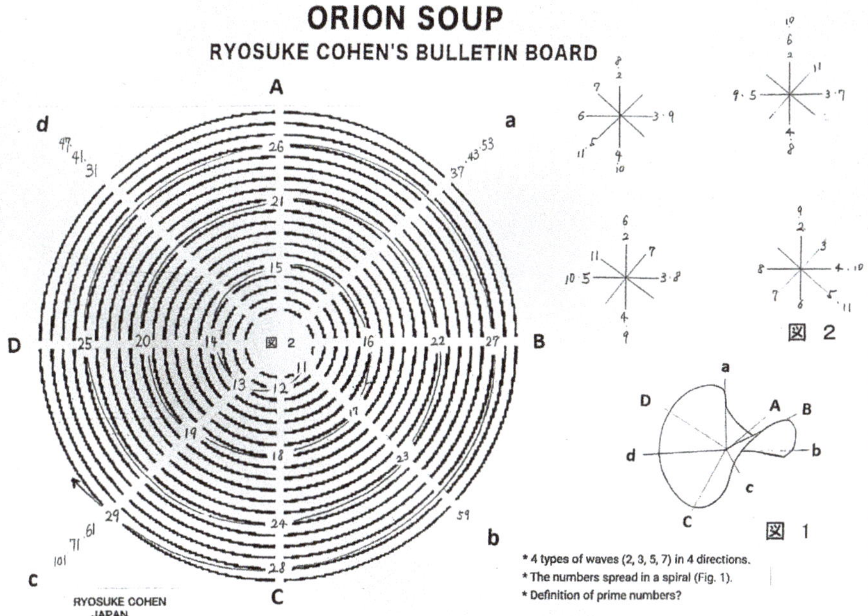

Orion Soup
Ryosuke Cohen, 2023

Serendipity-Doo!
Morgan Fisher, 2018

Hiyashi chūka (Chilled ramen)
Shikama Hiroko, 2018

ハム = ham　玉子 = egg

きうり = cucumber

はねりからし = mustard paste

Through sad or happy times
there's always been a cat

Gengorō, senryū poetry
Yamazaki Chidō, calligraphy, 2007
Barbara Summerhawk, translation, 2022

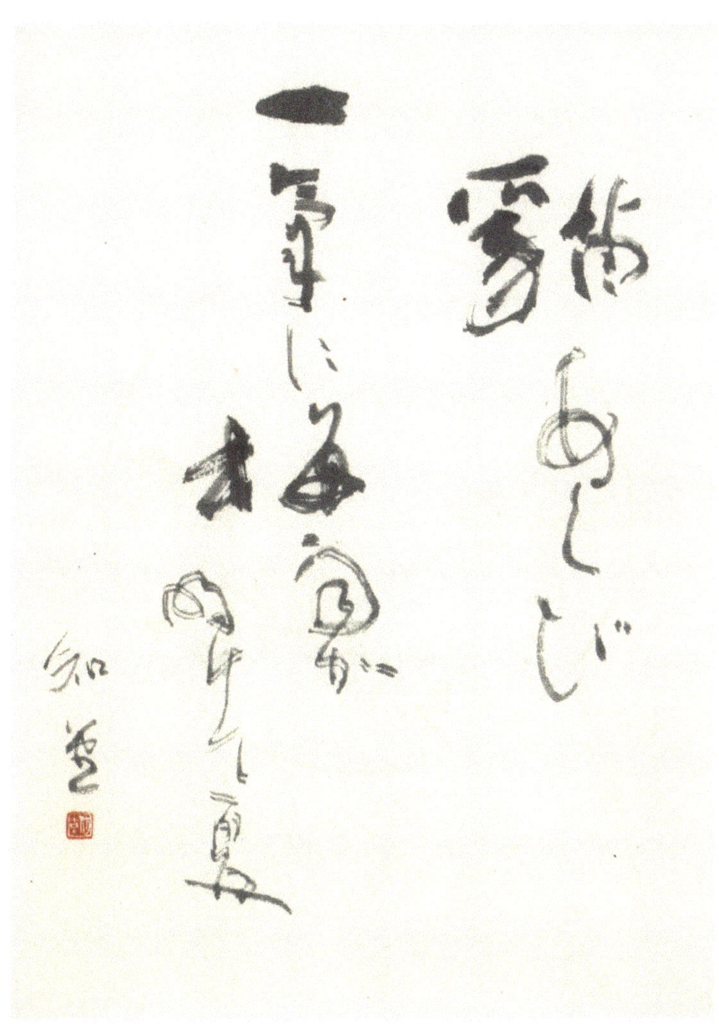

With one yawn from a cat
the rainy season blows into summer

Gengorō, senryū poetry
Yamazaki Chidō, calligraphy, 2007
Barbara Summerhawk, translation, 2022

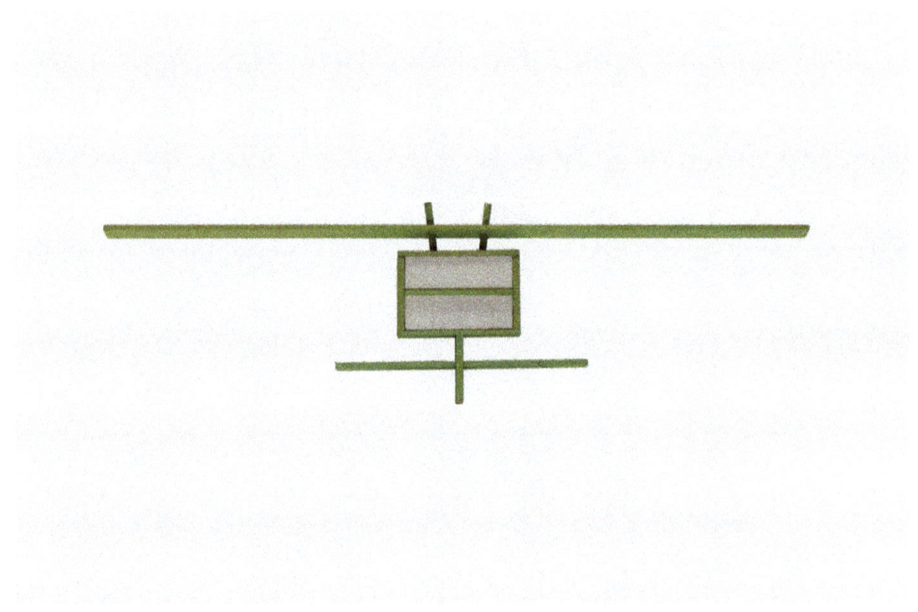

Kusa (grass)
Kunimine Teruko, 1980

AI-generated 3D poetry 1
Adachi Tomomi, 2023

AI-generated 3D poetry 2
Adachi Tomomi, 2023

AI-generated 3D poetry 3
Adachi Tomomi, 2023

ACKNOWLEDGMENTS

pp. 2, 5, 7 — Permission to use the lexical translations of Matsuo Bashō's haiku, "upon withered bough…" and "old pond!…," and of Kobayashi Issa's haiku, "faraway mountains…," was received from Adam L. Kern.

p. 3 — Permission to reprint "a winter crow…," by Nagata Koi, was granted by translator Margaret Mitsutani.

pp. 4, 37 — Permission to use *The Sound of Water* and *Self-portrait with the New York Times*, by Fujitomi Yasuo, was received from Mrs. Fujitomi Yasuko.

p. 8 — For use of Saitō Sanki's "A machine gun —," permission was kindly received from the translator Masaya Saito and Isobar Press.

p. 9 — For inclusion of Cid Corman's "A red thread…," permission was received from Bob Arnold, Literary Executor for the estate of Cid Corman.

p. 12 — Permission to reprint "Manifesto of The Japanese Futurist Movement" by Renkichi Hirato, was received from *Cabinet* magazine and translator Miryam Sas. The work was first printed in *Cabinet* no. 13, Spring 2004.

p. 14 — Design for Renkichi Hirato's *Ensemble* reconstructed by Rick Elizaga.

p. 15 — Permission to use Sho Sugita's translation of *Ensemble*, by Renkichi Hirato, from *Spiral Staircase*, was received from Ugly Duckling Presse.

p. 17 — Rick Elizaga contributed layout work to Kevin Shadel's translation of "View from a Balcony of an Early Summer Street" by Hagiwara Kyōjiro.

p. 25 — Layout for Andy Houwen's translation of Torii Ryōzen's "Wind's Glass" by Rick Elizaga.

pp. 30, 31, 32, 34 — Permission to publish Yamamoto Kansuke's poem, "Legend of a Buddhist Temple;" photo, *Buddhist Temple Birdcage;* poem, "Coup d'aujourd'hui;" and photo, *Under rose flowers of exploding black gunpowder / Girl flutters her braided hair running to the plaza / Dawn laughs out loud swaying its shoulders*; was received from Yamamoto Toshio.

pp. 30, 33 — Permission to publish the translations of the Yamamoto Kansuke poems, "Legend of a Buddhist Temple" and "Coup d'aujourd'hui," was gratefully received from John Solt.

pp. 42, 45 — Permission to reprint three of Kamimura Hiro's visual works from the broadside *Stillness* and Tanabu Hiroshi's three works from the broadside *Condition* was received from the holders of Karl Young's literary estate: Charles Alexander, Karl Kempton and Dan Waber.

p. 71 — Design for Aram Saroyan's *No title* reproduced by Rick Elizaga.

cover — Shikama Hiroko's photo manipulation of the Kūya sculpture incorporates a detail from Yamamoto Kansuke's "Under rose flowers...," p. 34.

SOURCES

Corman, Cid. "A red thread...," *Of*, Lapis Press, California, 1990.

Fujitomi Yasuo. *Shi wo miru: Nichidoku Bijuaru poetry han.* "Fujitomi Yasuo the sound of water." Gendaishika bungakukan. (*Texte sehen: Deutsche und Japanische Visuelle Poesie*. Fujitomi Yasuo, *the sound of water*. The Museum of Contemporary Poetry, Tanka and Haiku.) Iwate, 1999.

Fujitomi Yasuo. *Self-portrait with the* New York Times (highmoonoon broadside). "Celebrating the first exhibits of his drawings in Thailand." Undated.

Fukuda Kazuhiko. *Composition op. 75*, VOU 146, Tokyo, 1975.

Fukuda Kazuhiko. *Paper moon*, VOU 154, Tokyo, 1975.

Hagiwara Kyōjirō. "View from a Balcony of an Early Summer Street," from *Shikei senkoku* (Death sentence), 1925.

Kamimura Hiro. *Stillness* broadside. *Word/Light Pescia #2*, Light and Dust Books, Kenosha, Wisconsin, 1992.

Kempton, Karl. *A History of Visual Text Art.* Manchester/Berlin, Apple Pie Editions, 2018

Kern, Adam L. *The Penguin Book of Haiku.* Penguin Random House UK, 2018.

Nagata Koi. *A Dream Like This World: One Hundred Haiku* by Nagata Koi, translated by Margaret Mitsutani and Nana Naruto, 4-3-6, Toyosumi, Kashiwa, Chiba, 277-0071 Japan, 2000.

Renkichi Hirato, "Manifesto of the Japanese Futurist Movement" (translated by by Miryam Sas), *Cabinet* no. 13 Spring 2004.

Rossiter, Paul. *Monumenta Nipponica*, SARU Press, 1995.

Saitō Sanki. *Selected Haiku: 1933–1962*, translated by Masaya Saito. Isobar Press, 2023.

Shikama Hiroko. *Gui* 115, vol. 40, 2018.

Shōzō Torii. "World in My Pocket" (translated by Mignon), *Bearded Cones & Pleasure Blades: The Collected Poetry of Torii Shōzō*, highmoonoon, Hollywood, 2015.

Tanabu Hiroshi. *Condition* broadside. *Word/Light Pescia #3*, Light and Dust Books, Kenosha, Wisconsin, 1992.

Torii Ryōzen. *Poeme Graphique*, "Kaze no gurasu" (Wind's Glass), Kokubunsha, Tokyo, 1957.

Torii Ryōzen. *Katachi* (form), *VOU* 153, Tokyo, 1976.

Torii Ryōzen. *Witch*, *VOU* 154, Tokyo, 1977.

Tsuji Setsuko. *Shashinshu poeme:* < photo > Editions O, Tokyo, 1989.

Yamamoto Kansuke. "Coup d'aujourd'hui," from a series of seven postcards by Torii Shōzō, Kaijinsha, 1988. Originally published in *VOU* 70, 1959.

Yamamoto Kansuke. *Under rose flowers of exploding black gunpowder / Girl flutters her braided hair running to the plaza / Dawn laughs out loud swaying its shoulders*, 1983; *Japan's Modern Divide: The Photographs of Hiroshi Hamaya and Kansuke Yamamoto*, ed. by Judith Keller and Amanda Maddox, the J. Paul Getty Museum of Los Angeles, 2013.

Yoshizawa Shoji. *Oto kage* (Sound shadow) unnumbered broadside, Maru-7, Tokyo, 2003.

Photo of Taylor Mignon
by Ira Cohen
tagged by Ray Craig